Neglected Factors in
the Study of the Early
Progress of Christianity

✢ THE MORGAN LECTURES
DELIVERED IN THE THEOLOGICAL
SEMINARY OF AUBURN, IN THE
STATE OF NEW YORK, 1897 ✤ ✤

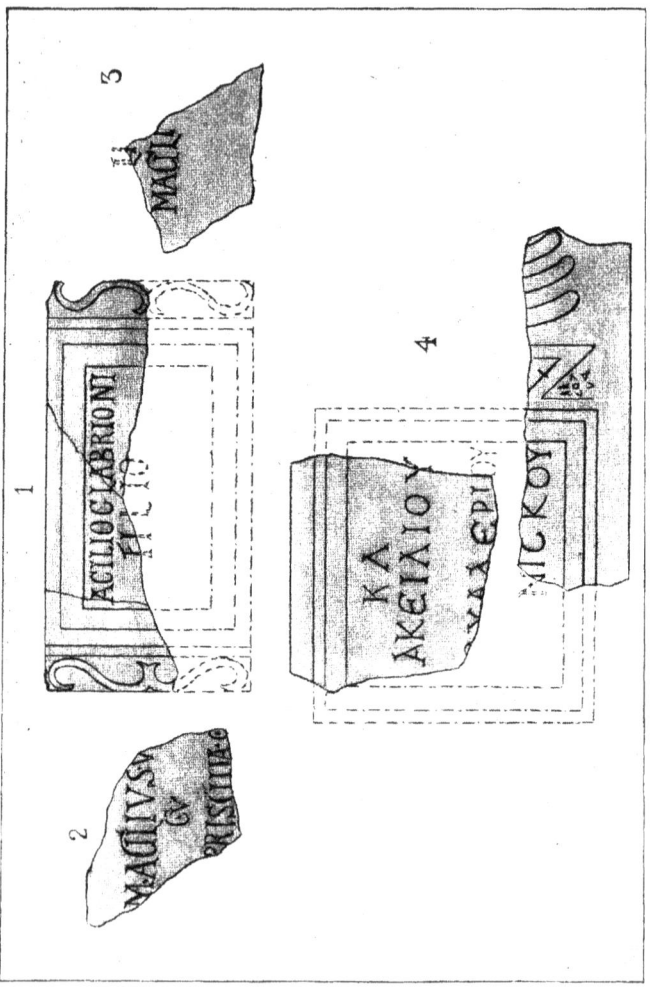

INSCRIPTIONS FOUND IN THE HYPOGEUM OF THE ACILII, CATACOMB OF PRISCILLA.

Neglected Factors in the Study of the Early Progress of Christianity. By the Rev. James Orr, D.D., *Professor of Church History in the United Presbyterian Theological College, Edinburgh* ✤ ✤ ✤ ✤ ✤

Wipf & Stock
PUBLISHERS
Eugene, Oregon

Wipf and Stock Publishers
199 W 8th Ave, Suite 3
Eugene, OR 97401

Neglected Factors in the Study of the Early Progress of Christianity
By Orr, James
ISBN: 1-59752-467-0
Publication date 2/16/2006
Previously published by Hodder and Stoughton, 1899

MORGAN LECTURES

Through the liberality of Mr. Henry A. Morgan, N.Y.S.

The three Lectures in this volume were originally prepared for the Mansfield Summer School, Oxford, 1894. They were delivered as the Morgan Lecture Course, in October, 1897, in the Theological Seminary of Auburn, in the State of New York. They are now published by request of the Faculty.

CONTENTS

LECTURE I

THE EXTENSION OF CHRISTIANITY LATERALLY OR NUMERICALLY IN THE ROMAN EMPIRE

PAGE

New spirit in Early Church studies—Baur and his successors—Influence of Pagan environment on Christianity—Less attention given to the action outward of Christianity on Paganism—The spread of Christianity *laterally, i.e.,* in respect of mere numbers, greater than ordinarily recognised — Estimates on this subject—Difficulties arising from fragmentariness of sources and unequal distribution of Christianity—The Catacombs a new factor—Results from Catacomb discoveries —Comparison with New Testament and other data—Early progress of the Church—Christianity in Asia Minor—The Apologists, &c. — Carthage — Alexandria — Antioch — Gibbon's objections—Gaul and Spain—The final struggle—General result . . . 13

LECTURE II

THE EXTENSION OF CHRISTIANITY VERTICALLY, OR AS RESPECTS THE DIFFERENT STRATA OF SOCIETY

Influence of Christianity on the higher ranks of society under-estimated — New Testament evidence — Witness of the Catacombs — Pomponia Græcina—Flavius Clemens and Domitilla — Acilius Glabrio — Notices in Second Century—The wealth of the Church of Rome—The witness of the persecutions — Tertullian and Clement on luxury of Christians—Relations of Christianity with the Imperial Court in the Third Century— The Decian persecution and its effects— The Church before and under Diocletian— Social status of Church teachers—Result: membership of the Early Church not drawn mainly from the lowest, but from the intermediate classes, and embraced many of the wealthier and higher orders 95

LECTURE III

THE INTENSIVE OR PENETRATIVE INFLUENCE OF CHRISTIANITY ON THE THOUGHT AND LIFE OF THE EMPIRE

The instreaming of Pagan influences on Christianity has for its counterpart the outstreaming of Christian influences on Pagan society—These also ordinarily under-estimated—Silence of Pagan writers: what it means—Christianity and culture in the First Century—New Testament Epistles—Seneca and the Gospel—Rise and character of Apology in the Second Century—The literary attack on Christianity : Celsus—Significance and spread of Gnosticism — The Pagan ethical revival in Second Century—Pagan preaching — Influence of Christianity on these—The Mysteries — The old Catholic Fathers—Rise of Neo-Platonism—Effects of Christianity on morals and legislation—Conclusion 163

APPENDIX 227

INDEX 231

THE EXTENSION OF CHRISTIANITY LATERALLY OR NUMERICALLY IN THE ROMAN EMPIRE

New spirit in Early Church studies—Baur and his successors—Influence of Pagan environment on Christianity—Less attention given to the action outward of Christianity on Paganism — The spread of Christianity *laterally*, *i.e.*, in respect of mere numbers, greater than ordinarily recognised—Estimates on this subject—Difficulties arising from fragmentariness of sources and unequal distribution of Christianity—The Catacombs a new factor—Results from Catacomb discoveries—Comparison with New Testament and other data—Early progress of the Church—Christianity in Asia Minor—The Apologists, &c. —Carthage — Alexandria — Antioch — Gibbon's objections—Gaul and Spain—The final struggle —General result.

LECTURE I

THE EXTENSION OF CHRISTIANITY *LATER-ALLY* OR *NUMERICALLY* IN THE ROMAN EMPIRE

IT is unnecessary at the commencement of these lectures to do more than refer to the changes which, within the last few decades, have taken place in the spirit and methods of the treatment of Church History. If there was a time within living memory when the charge could justly be brought against this branch of study of being the dreariest in the theological curriculum—a collection of dry bones and dead controversies—that time may confidently be said to have passed away; and with it has disappeared the idea that Church History must of necessity be an *unprogressive* science—the repetition of the old, unchanging story—seeing that the facts on which it is based must always remain precisely what they are. The changes referred to have come about not so much from the discovery of new materials—though of these also unremitting research has yielded an abundant supply—as from the new historical temper in which scholars have approached their task; from the fresh power acquired of reading aright the meaning of the data already possessed, and of setting them in new lights and relations; from increased skill in colligating them, and in interpreting the significance of unnoticed details in their bearing on an entire situation—in which lies so much of the higher art of

EARLY PROGRESS OF CHRISTIANITY 15

the historian. Just as the naturalist is reputed to be able from a single bone to reconstruct the form of some creature of the past, so our modern scholars aim at showing that the minutest fact is not isolated, but stands in organic relation with the all-pervading life of the time; and from comparison of the facts they seek to re-create for us a picture whose justification is its verisimilitude, and its power of interpreting the sum-total of the phenomena.

These gains which have accrued to Church History from the combined philosophical, historical, and critical movement of the last half century, have been reaped nowhere more largely than in the study of the earliest age of Christianity. The initial impulse here belongs indisputably to the school of Baur, which, however ruled by false pre-suppositions, and open to challenge in its conclusions, has left on this whole field of investigation its deep and abiding impress. If Baur's own criticism has gradually had to retract itself within comparatively narrow limits, it may claim, like the Nile waters, to have fertilised in the height of its overflow even the plains from which subsequently it had to retreat. From Baur's day a new life entered into Early Church History studies. Ritschl, at first a disciple, then an opponent, undertook an independent investigation into the origin of the Old Catholic Church; Lightfoot, not without aid from Ritschl, re-discussed the question of the Ministry, and cognate problems of the Apostolic age, but revealed also the unrivalled strength of his own scholarship in his handling of the literature of the age next succeeding; Hatch, freshest of English minds in this department, sought to show how Church ideas and usages took shape under the action of forces in the Gentile world; Harnack and the later Ritschlians have carried out more systematically the idea of the rise of ecclesiastical dogma through the importation of the ideas and methods of Greek philosophy; Neumann and Ramsay discuss the relations of the Christians to the Roman State, and the latter scholar has instituted a series of researches of his own, which mark a new era in the discussion of Apostolic and sub-Apostolic history. Other names, as Weizsäcker's, will readily occur. From this re-digging of the soil in all directions and microscopic scrutiny of every fibre and detail of the relevant material, it is impossible to doubt that enormous advantage will result.

There is, however, one aspect of this noteworthy revival of interest in Early Church History which the purpose of these lectures requires that I should now more particularly notice. It must strike the observant student —at least can hardly fail to do so when attention is called to it—that all this movement of mind in the direction of a better comprehension of the early development of the Church—of the manner in which it gradually shaped itself in policy, in doctrine, and in usages—is governed mainly by the idea of tracing the influence on Christianity of its Pagan environment—of that intellectual, moral, political, and religious environment, which constituted the world into which Christianity entered, and which could not from its very nature but powerfully act upon and modify the new faith ; but that the same attention has not been given to a phenomenon which is the counterpart of this, viz., the action outwards of Christianity on that Pagan environment, altering, re-shaping, modifying *it*. I am, of course, well aware that the action of Christianity on Pagan society—on its ideas, laws, institutions, morals—has in many of its aspects formed the subject of learned investigation.[1] But I do not find that it has been taken much account of in this most recent phase of the study of Early Church History which I have specially in view. There has been much investigation into the modes and the results of the inflow of Pagan ideas and associations into Christianity, but there has not been the same carefulness in inquiring whether the flow was all on one side, whether, as is antecedently probable, there was not a current *outward* corresponding to the current *inward*—to borrow a term from science, an exosmose corresponding to the endosmose— and what the strength of this outward current might be. It has not been sufficiently perceived—at least so I venture to think—that precisely in the proportion that the progress of investigation requires us to postulate a

[1] Such books may be referred to as Troplong's *De l'influence du Christianisme sur le droit civil des Romains*, Schmidt's *Social Results of Early Christianity*, Lecky's *European Morals*, Brace's *Gesta Christi*, &c.

greater influence of Paganism on Christian ideas and institutions than has formerly been assumed, there arises the probability, nay, the certainty, that Christianity likewise was a factor of greater importance in the world of Paganism than had previously been imagined, and that traces of this influence are also to be discovered, if they are as diligently looked for. Action and reaction, in this as in other spheres, may be presumed to be equal; and if the action is proved to be greater than former representations allowed, it may be anticipated that the reaction, in the case of a force of such undoubted magnitude, will prove to be greater as well.

I am now in a position to explain with some definiteness the character of the thesis I propose to defend in these lectures. I think facts do exist—and many of them—to show that there really was this current outwards of which I speak, and that Christianity was actually a much more prominent factor in Pagan society than the ordinary representations would lead us to believe; in other words, that just as the trend of investigation has been to show that there was a much greater influence of its Pagan environment upon the Church than has generally been conceded; so, correspondingly, the direction of recent evidence has been to establish that the effects of Christianity on Pagan society, both extensively and intensively, were likewise greater than has been admitted. I am fully conscious that in treating this subject I can say nothing that is new to scholars—little, perhaps, that is new to any one. The facts to which I am to refer are, most of them, sufficiently familiar—are, at the least, readily accessible; but we have hourly evidence that it is possible for a fact to be familiar, and yet not to receive its due weight in the study of a subject. It may help to disarm criticism if I say that, in what I advance, I desire to disclaim anything like dogmatism. I put forth these ideas tentatively, and rather with the view of their being canvassed and checked by others, than as definitive conclusions of my own mind. Their end will be gained if they are in any degree provocative of reflection in those who may honour them with their attention.

My treatment, which I should wish to be taken in its entirety, will be directed to show :—

I. That Christianity had a larger extension *laterally*, *i.e.*, in point of mere numbers, in the Roman Empire, than the ordinary representations allow.

II. That it had a much larger extension *vertically*, *i.e.*, as respects the different strata of society, than is commonly believed ; and—

III. That it had a much greater influence

intensively or *penetratively*, *i.e.*, in its effects on the thought and life of the age, than is generally acknowledged.

The remaining part of this lecture will be devoted to the first of these topics.

I.

The extension of Christianity *laterally* or *numerically* in the Roman Empire.

The attitude of mind of most historians on this question of the numerical extension of Christianity in the Roman world may be described as highly conservative. It is difficult to understand why this should be so, except that a prepossession in favour of a very moderate rate of increase having been engendered by the authority of certain great names, the feeling has established itself that this traditionally-received opinion ought not to be lightly disturbed. Whatever changes are assumed to be necessary in our conceptions of the relations of Christianity to Paganism in other respects, it is taken for granted with wonderful unanimity that there is neither room nor call for any revision of opinion here. Every one is familiar with Gibbon's estimate that the Christians in the time of Constantine constituted at most one-twentieth part of the population of Rome, and a like proportion of the whole subjects of the Empire.[1] Friedländer accepts and endorses this computation.[2] Chastel, a French writer, without, however, giving data,

[1] *Decline and Fall*, ch. xv. Gibbon estimates the population of Rome at about 1,000,000, and gives the Christians one-twentieth of these, or about 50,000. The population of the Empire he takes (ch. ii.) to be about 120,000,000, which would give about 6,000,000 Christians for the whole Empire. For other estimates of the population of Rome and the Empire, see V. Schultze's work referred to below, *Untergang des Heidenthums*, I. p. 9. Schultze computes 100,000,000 for the Empire, and, "with greatest probability," 600–810,000 for the Capital.

[2] *Sittengeschichte Roms*, III. p. 531.

reckons the Christians at about one-twelfth of the population,[1] and this, or one-tenth, perhaps, represents the average opinion. Victor Schultze, one of the best informed of recent investigators, estimates the proportion at one-tenth, but with important qualifications which practically nullify his verdict. "This reckoning," he says, "remains at all events far behind the actual number. . . . The investigator assuredly gains from the testing of the sources in detail the clear impression that, in the beginning of the fourth century, the Church on the great world-theatre of over 103,000 geographical square miles numbered more than 10,000,000. It is hardly credible that the number of Jews at that time should have exceeded that of

[1] One-fifteenth in the West, and one-tenth in the East.—*Hist. de la destruct. du Paganisme*, pp. 35–6. Chastel rejects Gibbon's computation as too low, and those of Staüdlin (one-half) and of Matter (one-fifth) as too high.

the Christians."[1] Others wisely decline to commit themselves to a precise estimate, still, however, usually with the presumption that the proportion was exceedingly small. Thus Uhlhorn scouts what he represents as Tertullian's statement that the Christians in a single province were more numerous than the whole Roman army, which, he says, as if it were an idea not for a moment to be entertained, would make about 9,000,000 Christians in the Empire![2]

In face of so weighty a consensus of authorities, I feel that it requires some courage to defend a different opinion. I am emboldened, however, by the considera-

[1] *Untergang des Griesch.-Röm. Heidenthums*, I. p. 23. Schultze is professor at Greifswald.

[2] *Conflict of Christianity* (E.T.), p. 264. Tertullian, however, does not quite put the matter in the way stated (*Apol.* 37). Uhlhorn says elsewhere : "It is generally assumed that they formed about one-twelfth of the whole population in the East, and in the West about one-fifteenth" (p. 402).

EARLY PROGRESS OF CHRISTIANITY 27

tion that in pleading for a much larger influence of Christianity numerically than these estimates allow, I do not stand absolutely alone. A few of the older writers, as Matter, put in a plea for one-fifth, or even a higher proportion, but their voices have scarcely been heard in the general chorus for a more moderate view. Still a tendency is beginning to manifest itself to a revision of the traditional estimate. Canon Robertson, among recent historians, apparently leans to a proportion between one-tenth and one-fifth.[1] And Keim, in his posthumous work, *Rom und das Christenthum*, expresses the belief that even at the close of the second century, the Christians were one-sixth of the population of the Empire.[2] G. Boissier, in his spirited book, *La Fin du Paganisme*,

[1] *Hist. of Church*, bk. 1, ch. viii.

[2] P. 419. "It is not saying too much," he writes, "to name a sixth part of the Roman Empire Christian."

speaks even more strongly on the arbitrariness of modern scholars, and their unwarrantable rejection of evidence on this subject. After quoting the well-known passages from Tertullian, Pliny, and Tacitus on the wide diffusion of Christianity, he says: "This is precisely what they (the objectors) refuse to admit. In the first place, they will take no account of the affirmations of Tertullian. He was, they say, a rhetorician and a sectary, facts which ought to render him doubly suspected. It would be ridiculous to take seriously his fine phrases, and give his rhetorical amplifications the force of argument. As for the letter of Pliny, and the passage in Tacitus, we have seen above that some do not believe them to be authentic, and the statements which they contain on the subject of the numbers of the Christians are one of the chief reasons alleged for rejecting them. There is found in them an exaggeration which betrays the forger, and appears altogether incredible. . . . It is proclaimed, finally, as a principle which needs no demonstration, that it is impossible that a religion should make such progress in so short a time. I confess that this confidence confounds me. Is it reasonable to settle in a word questions so obscure, so little understood?"[1] Even V. Schultze, as we saw above, is not very sure of his ground, and declares that the reckoning he gives remains far behind the actual numbers. Elsewhere, indeed, he uses language which would imply that the Christians, at the beginning of the fourth century, might be one-fifth, or even more, of the population.[2]

[1] I. pp. 445-46.
[2] Thus he speaks of the heathenism of the time as "over two-thirds of the population of the Empire"; again "as sixty or eighty millions out of one hundred millions"; and again of the Christians soon after the Edict of Toleration as "at most one-fifth of the population of the Empire" (I. pp. 39, 59).

Two things specially make it difficult to arrive at exact conclusions as to the number of Christians in the Roman Empire in this early period. One is the exceeding paucity and fragmentariness of our sources of information; the other is that the rate of progress in the different parts of the Empire was very unequal—much higher, *e.g.*, in the East than in the West; in Italy and North Africa than in a province like Gaul. "The imperfection of the record," as geologists would say, must ever be remembered. We shall find as we proceed abundant illustration of the danger of drawing wide inferences from isolated data, or of supposing that because nothing happens to be said of the progress of Christianity in a particular district, therefore progress was not being made. The second century, for instance, is already approaching its close before we get even a glimpse of the large and flourishing Church of Carthage,

EARLY PROGRESS OF CHRISTIANITY 31

which, with the Church of Alexandria, then suddenly starts into visibility.[1] On the other hand, the rate of progress was undoubtedly very unequal, and even more instructive than the inequality of progress is the fact which furnishes the principal explanation of it. It is characteristic of the advance of Christianity that all through it struck at the great centres, and followed the great lines of intercommunication in the Roman world; that its chief victories were won where Greek and Roman culture had prepared the way for it; and that its posts of strength and influence were chiefly in the wealthy and populous

[1] "Of the African Church before the close of the second century, when a flood of light is suddenly thrown up by the writings of Tertullian, *we know absolutely nothing*" (Lightfoot, *Philippians*, p. 224). Another example is Cyrene, where the size and adornment of the graves show the existence of a numerous and well-to-do community, of which we do not hear otherwise (Cf. V. Schultze, I. p. 21). In the troubles of the times this church afterwards fell into decay.

cities—Rome, Corinth, Antioch, Alexandria, Carthage, Lyons, and the like—from which it could spread into, and best dominate, the surrounding districts.[1] Its method—the same followed by Paul in his missionary work—was to seize and occupy the leading vantage-points, with a view to an ultimate wider diffusion. Numbers, then, in a case of this kind, are assuredly not everything. As important as numbers was the way in which the numbers were distributed, and the spirit that animated them. It is not overlooked by the writers from whose opinions we shall have to dissent, that, though numerically so feeble,—as they regard the matter,—Christianity had yet, through its inherent spiritual energy, and ever-strengthening organisation, early made itself a factor of the first importance in the Roman Empire,—that, as Merivale says,

[1] Cf. V. Schultze, I. p. 15; Ramsay, *Church in Roman Empire*, p. 147 (1st edit.), &c.

EARLY PROGRESS OF CHRISTIANITY 33

"The active and growing strength of the Roman world was truly theirs—theirs was the future of all civilised society."[1] But the question is pertinent whether this acknowledged power of Christianity could have been exerted by the mere fraction of the population which they suppose the Christian Church to have been; or whether the immense moral energy which, at the end of three centuries, and on the back of a prolonged and deadly persecution, raised the Church to a place of undisputed political supremacy in the Empire, does not of itself point to some fault in the numerical estimate. I cannot, of course, in a brief lecture, go into all the evidence. I can only take test cases, which fairly represent large areas, and may serve to illustrate principles.

Now that there is need for some revisal of currently received notions on the rate

[1] *Epochs of Early Church History*, p. 2.

of progress of early Christianity is shown, I think, very convincingly by one branch of evidence, the full bearings of which on our subject seem as yet to be very imperfectly appreciated. I refer to the remarkable Catacomb explorations of De Rossi and others in the present century. It is customary to discount the glowing testimonies of the second century Apologists, and of early Christian writers generally, on the score of rhetorical exaggeration; but here, opened to us within recent years, is another book of surpassing interest, the pages of which are constantly being more clearly deciphered by skilled interpreters, and which promises to throw a flood of reliable light on just such problems as we are dealing with. It is surprising that these discoveries have not been made more use of by Church historians.[1] Their effect, I

[1] Dr. Schaff speaks of the importance of these discoveries, and notes the neglect of them by Church

take it, must be largely to modify our ideas of the numbers of the Christians, and to compel the acknowledgment that they formed a much larger proportion of the population of the Empire than has hitherto been suspected. It will be convenient to take this new evidence first, then to ask how far it is corroborated or contradicted by the other evidence at our command.

The Catacombs, as most are now aware are immense subterranean burial-places, excavated in the soft volcanic tufa, near the great roads, within a radius of about three miles around Rome. There are certain facts regarding them which may now be regarded as definitely ascertained.[1] They

historians. He himself gives a good account of them, but makes little use of their testimony in the body of his work. He mentions their witness to the numbers of the Christians, but does not well know what to make of it.—*History of Church* (Ante-Nic.), Preface, and pp. 288, 295.

[1] The name, of doubtful derivation, was originally

are allowed to be Christian, and purely Christian cemeteries[1]; they are of enormous extent; the number of the dead buried in them mounts up to millions; the time allowed for this burial is about three centuries — in reality, little more than two centuries and a half, for the excavations had hardly begun before the second century and the numbers interred after the middle of the fourth century were small in proportion to those in the preceding period. After the sack of Rome by the Goths in A.D. 410, interment within them ceased. The excava-

that of a territory adjacent to the cemetery of St. Sebastian, and only subsequently was extended to all the cemeteries. Over forty catacombs are enumerated — twenty-five or twenty-six greater, the rest smaller. For particulars see the works (in English) of Northcote and Brownlow, Lanciani, Withrow, Art. in *Dictionary of Christian Antiquities*, Black's *Handbook to Christ. and Ecc. Rome*, &c.

[1] Northcote and Brownlow, I. p. 376; *Dict. of Christ. Antiquities*, I. p. 296; Northcote's *Epitaphs*, pp. 22 ff.

EARLY PROGRESS OF CHRISTIANITY 37

tions consist of galleries and chambers, sometimes in descending levels of from three to five stories, and throughout their entire area are literally packed with graves, the dead being sometimes buried in the floors, as well as in the walls and rooms. What is not so certain is the precise figure to be put on their extent, or on the number of the dead interred in them. On these points estimates widely vary. The most careful and reliable calculations are those of Michele Stefano de Rossi, brother and coadjutor of the famous explorer, who, on the basis of the exact measurement of six different catacombs, reckons the total length of the passages at 587 geographical miles.[1] As respects the numbers entombed,

---

[1] See the details of measurements in Lanciani's *Pagan and Christian Rome*, p. 319. Northcote and Brownlow, *Roma Sott.* I. p. 2, give the apparently conflicting estimate of "more than 350 miles." But the appended words, "*i.e.*, more than the whole length of Italy itself," show that the same calcula-

38 NEGLECTED FACTORS IN THE

we may set aside at once as fabulous the earlier computation of Father Marchi, who calculating the length of the passages at 900 miles, reckoned the dead interred in them at 7,000,000![1] A less extravagant calculation gives over 3,831,000, or nearly 4,000,000 graves.[2] Michele de Rossi, who has had most to do with the surveying and mapping out of these subterranean regions, adopting a more moderate multiplier, reaches a *minimum* of 1,752,000.[3] Now let any one

tion is intended, and the 350 is either a misprint for 550, or there is some other confusion about the numbers.

[1] Dr. Schaff amazingly accepts this computation of Father Marchi's in speaking of the number of the martyrs (I. p. 80), in complete contradiction of his calculation of the numbers of the Christians elsewhere.

[2] See Withrow, p. 21. He mentions that "in the single crypt of St. Lucina, 100 ft. by 180 ft., De Rossi counted over 700 *loculi*, and estimated that nearly twice as many were destroyed, giving a total of 2,000 graves in this area."

[3] Lanciani, *ut supra*.

EARLY PROGRESS OF CHRISTIANITY 39

reflect what computations like these imply. Taking the period of interment at its longest, we cannot count more than ten generations of Christians buried in the Catacombs. Assuming that the numbers are anything like what the above computations indicate, we obtain from them the basis of a simple, but sufficiently startling calculation. On the larger reckoning—that of about 4,000,000 graves—we have a Christian population for one generation, in and about Rome, of nearly 400,000; on the smaller computation, a population of about 175,000. But the system of averages in such a case is clearly misleading, for the number of Christians was undoubtedly small in the earlier generations, and reached its maximum towards the close of the era of persecution. Our number 175,000 would, therefore, represent rather a middle point, say, about the years A.D. 230 or 250. Compare this now with the calculation of Gibbon.

He estimates, as we saw, the population of Rome at about 1,000,000, and the number of Christians at the beginning of the fourth century at about 50,000, or one-twentieth part of the whole. In reality, unless the testimony of the Catacombs has been totally misread, they might have been anything between one-third and one-half. And if Gibbon is right in supposing that the proportion throughout the Empire was analogous to that in Rome, it would be a very moderate computation indeed to regard it as one-fifth. In any case, it seems to me, there must be a heightening of the reckoning. Cut down the figures even to 1,000,000 and the proportion of Christians to the total population is still vastly greater than Gibbon allows. I think, therefore, I am justified in speaking of the Catacomb discoveries as a "neglected factor" in this study of Early Church History—one which only recently Church historians have taken the trouble to refer to at all, and of the bearings of which even yet they show generally a most inadequate appreciation. I go on to ask whether there is anything in the other evidence in our possession which helps to corroborate, or which contradicts, the testimony they have yielded.

I begin naturally with the Church of Rome, to which the Catacomb discoveries refer. Our witnesses here are the New Testament, and early secular and ecclesiastical history. And what do these witnesses tell us? The facts above cited are sufficiently startling, but are they really more wonderful than the oldest notices we possess of the progress of the gospel in the Imperial City would lead us to expect? The origin of the Church in Rome is hidden in obscurity, but there are certain things about its early history which we do know very well. We know, for instance, that as early as A.D. 52, or little more that twenty years after the Ascension, according to the now almost universally received interpretation of the well-known passage in Suetonius *(Judæos impulsore Chresto assidue tumultuantes Roma expulit)*, the disturbances in the Jewish quarters in Rome, arising from the disputes of Jews and Christians, were such as to lead the Emperor Claudius to issue an edict for the banishment of all Jews from Rome[1]; we know that six years later (A.D. 58), and prior to his own visit to the city, the Apostle Paul wrote to the Church in this city one of his longest and most important Epistles, in which he speaks of its faith as "proclaimed throughout the whole

[1] Suet. *Claud.* 25; cf. Acts xviii. 2. "Probably the measures which the Emperor took against the Roman Jews had their origin in the continual disturbances arising from the strife between Jews and Christians" (Neumann, *Der Römische Staat*, p. 4). Thus most writers. Prof. Ramsay puts the date a little earlier, A.D. 50 (*St. Paul the Traveller*, ch. xi. 4).

EARLY PROGRESS OF CHRISTIANITY 43

world"[1]; we know that six years later again (A.D. 64), according to the testimony of the Roman historian Tacitus, the number of the Christians involved in Nero's persecution was "an immense multitude" *(multitudo ingens)*[2]; while, towards the close of the century, the Roman Clement, referring to the same persecution, uses an almost identical expression, speaking of "a great multitude" ($\pi o\lambda \grave{v} \; \pi \lambda \hat{\eta} \theta o\varsigma$) who had suffered for Christ.[3] All this, be it

---

[1] Rom. i. 8; cf. Lightfoot, *Philippians*, p. 25.

[2] *Ann*. xv. 44. Schultze remarks that the *multitudo ingens* is of those taken and condemned, and that there was certainly as great a number of women, children, and other Christians who were not brought to judgment (I. 9). Cf. Dr. Lightfoot's remarks on the attempts of modern critics to invalidate the force of this testimony of Tacitus (*Ignatius*, I. pp. 9-10).

[3] *Epist. to Corinth.* 6. The progress of Christianity was more than maintained during the rest of the century. "During the reigns of Vespasian and Titus, and in the early years of Domitian, there is every reason to believe that Christianity had made rapid advances in the metropolis of the world. In its

remembered, within the first century, when Catacomb excavations had yet hardly begun. And what was going on in Rome in this century was, we have no reason to doubt, going on elsewhere. I cannot go into details, but would only ask whether Christianity must not have become an exceedingly powerful force before, in a city like Ephesus, for example, we could have the adepts in magical arts bringing their books, and burning them to the value of 50,000 pieces of silver [1]; or have a riot like that instigated by Demetrius the silversmith, on the plea that not only the trade of shrine-making was brought into disrepute, but the worship of the great goddess Artemis was in peril of being subverted " not

great stronghold—the household of the Cæsars—more especially its progress would be felt" (Lightfoot, *Clement*, I. p. 27).

[1] Acts xix. 18, 19. About £2,000 of our money. "So mightily grew the word of the Lord and prevailed" (ver. 20).

EARLY PROGRESS OF CHRISTIANITY 45

alone at Ephesus, but almost throughout all Asia"[1]; or whether things must not have gone far to justify even a hyperbole like Paul's that the gospel had been "preached in all creation under heaven," and was "also in all the world bearing fruit and increasing"[2]; or, finally, to furnish a basis for the pictures in the Apocalypse of the "great multitude which no man could number, out of every nation, and of all tribes and peoples and tongues," which had "come out of the great tribulation"?[3]

Darkness rests upon the closing decades of the first century, but we have the testimony from the early part of the next century of the newly recovered *Apology of Aristides*, which relates how, after the Lord's Ascension, His twelve disciples "went forth into the known parts [*Gr.* provinces] of the world,

---

[1] Vers. 23–27.　　[2] Col. i. 6, 23 (R.V.).
[3] Rev. vii. 9.　Cf. Lightfoot, *Philippians*, p. 25.

and taught concerning His greatness"[1]; and through the dim mists of tradition we can descry the figures of these Apostles spread over the various countries of the world—in Parthia and Scythia, on the bleak shores of the Euxine, in Mesopotamia, in Arabia, perhaps as far even as India—and can catch glimpses which show that the work of evangelisation was actively going on.[2] When the curtain lifts again in the second century, we have many indications, direct and indirect, of the immense advances that had been made. I do not dwell on what Gibbon calls the

[1] *Apology*, 2. The *Apology* has usually been ascribed, after Eusebius, to the reign of Hadrian (about A.D. 125–6); but a second title in the Syriac has led Prof. Rendel Harris and other scholars to place it later, under Antoninus. Mr. Armitage Robinson, however, prefers the older view (*Texts and Studies*, I. p. 75).

[2] The best examination of these traditions is probably that of Lipsius in his article on "Acts of Apostles (Apocryphal)," in Smith and Wace's *Dict. of Christian Biog.*, I. pp. 17–32.

"splendid exaggeration" of Justin Martyr, who declares: "For there is not one single race of men, whether barbarians, or Greeks, or whatever they may be called, nomads, or vagrants, or herdsmen dwelling in tents, among whom prayers and giving of thanks are not offered through the name of the Crucified Jesus,"[1]—though if one reflects that Justin does not claim that all the races or tribes he speaks of had been converted to the gospel, or were even preponderatingly Christian, but only that the gospel had reached them, and had won from each its tribute of believers, the exaggeration need not be so great after all—but proceed at once to the examination of more particular evidence.

[1] *Dial. cum Tryph.*, c. 117; cf. Gibbon, ch. xv. Mosheim remarks, "There could have been no room for this very exaggeration, had not the Christian religion at that time been most extensively diffused throughout the world" (*Commentaries*, I. p. 260, E.T.).

The case which naturally first arrests our attention here is that of Asia Minor, in regard to an extensive province of which we are exceptionally fortunate in having the unimpeachable testimony of Pliny, Pro-consul of Bithynia-Pontus, in his famous letter to the Emperor Trajan (A.D. 112). This letter of Pliny is a remarkable warning at the outset of the danger of reliance on the mere argument from silence; for, but for its existence, it is certain that the actual state of the case in this province would not have been known to us, and could hardly have been conjectured or believed.[1] Had

---

[1] "Tertullian derived his knowledge of it from the correspondence of Pliny and Trajan; Eusebius from Tertullian; later Christian writers from Tertullian and Eusebius, one or both. The correspondence of a heathen writer is thus the sole ultimate chronicle of this important chapter in the sufferings of the Early Church" (Lightfoot, *Ignatius*, I. p. 18; cf. Ramsay, *Church in Roman Empire*, pp. 146, 196). Ramsay mentions that the text of the letter depends

EARLY PROGRESS OF CHRISTIANITY 49

any Christian writer, *e.g.*, chosen to put it on record that at this early date in the second century the Christian religion was already professed by "many of all ages and ranks, and of both sexes" (*multi omnis ætatis, omnis ordinis, utriusque sexus etiam*) throughout this extensive region; that the movement was "not confined to the cities, but had spread into the villages and country" (*neque enim civitates tantum, sed vicos etiam atque agros*); that the temples of the heathen were "almost deserted" (*prope jam desolata templa*); that the "sacred rites" were "interrupted" (*solemnia intermissa*); that the victims for sacrifice could find "very few purchasers" (*rarissimus auctor inveniebatur*); and that this had been going on for a long time (*diu*), I fancy we should have been disposed to accuse him, as we

on a single manuscript, found in 1500, used in 1508, and never since seen or known.

do Justin and Tertullian, of rhetorical exaggeration.[1] It is different when these statements appear in a cool official document, written expressly to obtain guidance in the discharge of proconsular duty. What makes the testimony of Pliny the more valuable is the wide extent of territory to which his witness applies. From recent authorities[2] we learn that the region over which Pliny's jurisdiction extended stretched far to the east; that it included the district known as Pontus, and had in fact for its correct designation the Province of Bithynia *and* Pontus; and that Pliny was probably in the east or Pontic part of it when he wrote to Trajan. His description, therefore, will include Pontus as well as other parts of the province. This is corroborated

[1] The text of the letter may be seen in Lightfoot's *Ignatius*, and in works on Church History generally.

[2] Mommsen, quoted by Ramsay, p. 224; Lightfoot's *Ignatius*, p. 56.

by Lucian, the friend of Celsus, who, writing after the middle of the century, makes his hero, Alexander of Abonotichus, describe his native country, Pontus, as "filled with Epicureans and Christians."[1] We have besides numerous notices of the Churches of Pontus in Eusebius.[2] Yet Bithynia and Pontus, though already possessing Christian communities when Peter wrote his First Epistle, were not among the parts of Asia Minor favoured with Paul's labours. In this connection we come on another interesting fact—important, as again warning us against drawing wide inferences from fragmentary data to the prejudice of the progress of Christianity. Here in the second century we have indubitable evidence that Pontus was swarming with Christians. Yet

[1] Lucian, *Alex.*, c. 25. Quoted by Gibbon, Mosheim, Schultze, &c.

[2] Bk. iv. 15, 23; v. 16, 23; viii. 12, &c.

in the biography of Gregory Thaumaturgus, Origen's pupil, written by his namesake, Gregory of Nyssa — a century after his death it is true, and with many fabulous adornments—it is told that when Gregory was made Bishop of Neo-Cæsarea, in Pontus, in A.D. 240 [not the Pontus of Pliny, but in its immediate neighbourhood], he found only seventeen Christians.[1] It is added, by way of preserving the symmetry, that when he died he left only seventeen pagans! The conversion of the district was thus accomplished at least within the third century. But how unsafe it would be to argue from the alleged paucity of Christians in A.D. 240, in Pontus—which, if real, must have been due to local causes—to the general condition of Pontus earlier!

We are not yet done, however, with Asia Minor. There is no reason that I know of,

[1] Migne, xlvi. p. 954.

EARLY PROGRESS OF CHRISTIANITY 53

beyond the fact that we have not a Pliny to describe them, for supposing that what was true of Bithynia and Pontus, was not true of many other provinces as well. There is every reason for supposing that some of these provinces were even more favourably situated. In Phrygia, *e.g.*, the seat of the outbreak of Montanism, Christianity must have been very strong. Renan says boldly: " In Hierapolis, and many towns of Phrygia, the Christians must have formed the majority of the population."[1] The recent discovery of the singularly

---

[1] *Marc-Aurèle*, p. 449; so in his *Saint Paul* (chap. xiii.), "Phrygia was thenceforward, and remained for 300 years, a Christian country." Cf. Ramsay, *Church in Roman Empire*, pp. 146-7. Renan mentions that from the time of Septimus Severus, Apameia, of Phrygia, put on its coins a Biblical emblem, Noah's Ark. Prof. Ramsay takes this to be Jewish (*Cities and Bishoprics of Phrygia*, II. p. 670). This last-named work of Prof. Ramsay's contains much new matter and evidence from inscriptions on the power of Christianity in certain districts of Phrygia. (See specially vol. ii., chaps. xii. and xvii.) "To judge

interesting epitaph of Abercius, of Hierapolis,[1] identified with the Avircius Marcellus, known to us from Eusebius as a prominent opponent of Montanism,[2] sheds light on the presence of Christianity in the Phrygian Pentapolis. Western Asia, with its historical churches, and traditions of St. John, would not be far

from the proportion of epitaphs, the population of Eumeneia in the third century was in great part Christian. . . . These facts show that Eumeneia was to a large extent a Christian city during the third century. . . . It is clear that, for some reason, Christianity spread to quite an extraordinary extent in Eumeneia and Apameia" (pp. 502, 511).

[1] Cf. Lightfoot, *Ignatius*, I. pp. 447–86, and Prof. Ramsay (to whom belongs the chief merit of this discovery) in *Cities and Bishoprics of Phrygia*, II., chap. xvii. "All that is known of the history of the Pentapolis," he says, "centres round the name of Avircius Marcellus. He is presented to us as the most prominent Church leader in a district already permeated with Christian influence, and the chief figure in the resistance to Montanism in the latter part of the second century. . . . That the Pentapolis was Christianised very early is plain from the facts above stated" (pp. 709, 715).

[2] *Ecc. Hist.*, v. 16.

EARLY PROGRESS OF CHRISTIANITY 55

behind.[1] I do not touch on the vexed question of North or South Galatia—though renewed study has failed to reconcile me to what I conceive to be the superior improbabilities of the hypothesis to which Prof. Ramsay has lent his powerful advocacy[2]—

[1] Cf. Lightfoot's essay on "The Later School of St. John," in *Essays on Super. Religion.* The Epistles of Ignatius, and scenes like the Martyrdom of Polycarp, are in evidence here to the existence of numerous and well-organised Christian churches.

[2] Prof. Ramsay lays, perhaps, too much stress on the ignorance of Greek in North Galatia, and on the suppression of the Phrygian element in the population (e.g., *Church in Roman Empire,* pp. 79, 82, 99). Mommsen does not take so strong a view. A good portion of the inhabitants, he says, "must have descended from the older Phrygian inhabitants of these regions. Of still more weight is the fact that the zealous worship of the gods in Galatia and the priesthood there have nothing in common with the ritual institutions of the European Celts ; not merely was the Great Mother, whose sacred symbol the Romans of Hannibal's time asked and received from the Tolistobogi, of a Phrygian type, but her priests belonged in part at least to the Galatian nobility ['Phrygo-Galatic,' surely.] . . . As the language of

but in any case Ancyra, in Galatia, was a prominent Church in the middle of the second century,[1] and the gospel was, no doubt, diffused through the province then as elsewhere. In Cappadocia there was from early times a powerful Christian community. V. Schultze finds in the fourth century "the power of heathenism longer broken" in that province, "than anywhere else in the world," and "the majority of the inhabitants" of the chief city Christian.[2] At the Council of Nice,

---

conversation, the Celtic maintained its grounds with tenacity also in Asia, yet the Greek gradually gained the upper hand," &c. (*Provinces of Roman Empire*, I. p. 341). The topographical difficulties may be great, but, in our ignorance of the whole circumstances, can hardly be said to be insuperable, and they are not all on one side. Prof. Ramsay's own pages show how precarious it is to argue from absence or paucity of inscriptions (*Cities and Bishoprics*, II. pp. 484, 491, 499–502, &c.). The rival probabilities, however, cannot be discussed here.

[1] Eus. v. 16.

[2] *Untergang des Heid.*, II. p. 315. See the numerous references in Eusebius.

EARLY PROGRESS OF CHRISTIANITY 57

in 325, the bishops of Asia Minor formed about a third of the total number.[1] Compare now these facts with Schultze's own estimate that the Christians in Asia Minor in Constantine's time may have amounted to 1,000,000, out of a total population of 19,000,000,[2] or about one-nineteenth part, and it will probably be felt that the estimate is altogether inadequate. The proportion may more reasonably be assumed to be not dissimilar to that we have already met with in Rome.

It may be held, however, that Asia Minor is an exceptionally favourable case for our argument, and this may well be so. Our

[1] Cf. the list in Schultze, II. pp. 305-7. It may be noted that five bishops are named from churches in (North) Galatia, and seven from Pamphylia (with Lycia)—another region of which we are apt to infer from silence that it had no church-life of importance.

[2] I. p. 18. Of course this is a minimum, and Schultze's important qualifications have to be remembered.

knowledge of the state and progress of the Church during the greater part of the second century is exceedingly fragmentary; yet putting together the pieces of evidence which we possess—the numerous references, *e.g.*, to a chronic state of persecution in Justin and other Apologists [1]; the rise of Apology itself, as bearing witness to the growing importance of the Church, and its entrance into literary circles [2]; the edicts and rescripts of emperors on the treatment of the Christians, some of them embracing a wide area [3]; the extraordinarily rapid development and propagation of Gnostic errors — multiplying, as

[1] See references in Lightfoot, *Ignatius*, I. pp. 518 ff.
[2] On this and the rise of Gnosticism, see Lecture III.
[3] Those of Hadrian, Antoninus, and M. Aurelius; cf. Lightfoot, *Ignatius*, I. pp. 461 ff. The passage from Melito (Eus. iv. 26) on letters of Antoninus to the cities forbidding them to take any new measures against the Christians, " among the rest to the Larissæans, to the Thessalonians, to the Athenians, and to all the Greeks," deserves special notice.

Irenæus says, like mushrooms out of the ground [1]; the vivid light-flashes which illuminate such martyr-scenes as those of Ignatius of Antioch, of the venerable Polycarp of Smyrna, of Justin and his companions at Rome, of the Martyrs of Vienne and Lyons,[2] and serve to reveal how much there is to see if only we had light enough to see it—piecing these notices together, we may find good reason for believing that, with the exception of outlying regions like those of Gaul and Germany, the state of matters in the other parts of the Roman world was not essentially different from what we have already found. Celsus dreads the growing numbers of the Christians, and writes an elaborate book to ridicule and refute them [3]; and Eusebius, looking back

[1] *Ad. Hær.*, bk. i. 29.

[2] Cf. Eus. iii. 36; iv. 15, 16; v. 1; and cf. Lightfoot on incidents.

[3] Cf. Uhlhorn's *Conflict of Christianity* (E.T.), p. 279; and see Lecture III.

upon the period, speaks of Christianity as spreading at this time so as to embrace the whole human race.[1]

I do not wait on these general considerations, but pass to the close of the second century, when light fully returns to us, and we are able to see how immense a progress has been made. We are now in the age of the Old Catholic Fathers, and find ourselves confronted with a great and firmly-organised Church, claiming to be "Catholic and Apostolic," spread throughout the chief provinces of the Empire, and waging a victorious conflict with Gnosticism and Montanism on the one side, and Paganism on the other. Now for the first time the important Churches of Carthage and Alexandria come fully into view. Only now, as formerly observed, do we gain a hint of the existence of a Church in the former of these

[1] Eus. iv. 7.

cities. It is as when a traveller, at a sharp turning of his road, suddenly finds himself in presence of a busy and populous city, the very name of which had previously been unknown to him. Yet both Churches are discovered to be already of long standing; both are wealthy and numerically prosperous; both have to bear the brunt of the greater persecutions; in both the crowds of the lapsed in the hour of trial reveal at once the high social position of many of the converts, and the nominal character of much of their profession.

The situation in Carthage is vividly depicted for us in the pages of the fiery and eloquent Tertullian. There is no longer any mistaking the fact that, notwithstanding the numerical inferiority of the Christians, and the severe persecutions by which it was sought to restrain them, the flowing tide was with the new faith, and the heathen themselves were profoundly alarmed at its progress. "Men cry out," says the Apologist, "that the State is besieged; the Christians are in the fields, in the forts, in the islands; they mourn, as for a loss, that every sex, age, condition, and even rank, is going over to this sect"[1]; and he tells us, in language resembling Pliny's, "the temple revenues are every day falling off; how few now throw in a contribution."[2] This is rhetoric, no doubt, but we do not feel it necessary to set it aside wholly as the language of exaggeration. It is only what the facts before us would lead us to expect. In his address to the Proconsul Scapula in deprecation of the persecutions of the Christians—to a man, therefore, who must have been able to detect any extravagant exaggeration—Tertullian asserts boldly, "Though our numbers are so great—*constituting all but a majority in every city (pars*

[1] *Apol.* 1.   [2] C. 42.

pene major civitatis cujusque)—we conduct ourselves in quietness and modesty "[1]; and says again that if the Christians in Carthage were to present themselves in a body before his tribunal, he would have to decimate the city to make an example of them.[2] Tertullian, we allow again, was a rhetorician, but there was at least some method in his rhetoric, and it would plainly have defeated the very end he had in view had he addressed an appeal to a proconsul, intended to influence his action, which was on the face of it monstrously and even ludicrously at variance with the facts. It is in the light of state-

[1] *Ad. Scap.* 2.
[2] C. 5. If one wishes to press the "decimate" of the rhetorician, as implying that the numbers whom he had just described as "all but a majority in every city," constituted literally and exactly one-tenth, it may be observed that it is only the adult part of the community that would figure in such a scene as this, and *all* need not be conceived of as massacred.

ments like these, where a certain caution—not to say verisimilitude—must have been employed, that we must judge of his other celebrated outburst in the Apology, "We are but of yesterday, and yet we have filled every place belonging to you—cities, islands, castles, towns, assemblies, your very camps, your tribes, companies, palace, senate, forum —we leave you your temples only."[1] Neumann justly remarks that, to prove effective, such statements must have been able to attach themselves to known facts.[2] It is a

[1] C. 37.

[2] *Der Römische Staat*, p. 121. So Hasenclever, in his able articles on the social rank of the early Christians in *Jahr. f. Prot. Theol.*, viii., speaks of Tertullian's rhetorical exaggeration as "essentially agreeable to the fact" (p. 36). There is more reason for supposing that Tertullian gives wings to his imagination in his enumeration of the various nations that had received the gospel (*Ad. Jud.* 7); but even this passage is only an expansion of similar statements in Justin and Irenæus. The latter Father speaks of the Church in his day as "dispersed throughout the whole world, even to the ends of the earth," and enumerates the

EARLY PROGRESS OF CHRISTIANITY 65

very moderate interpretation, I think, to put upon them to say that the Christians by the end of the second century must have formed one-fifth or one-sixth of the population of the North African cities, and perhaps one-tenth of the whole province. Schultze, on the other hand, computes as a minimum only 50,000 out of a population of half a million in the city, or one-tenth, and a total of 100,000 in the province, or about 1 per cent.![1] A totally inadequate estimate, as it seems to me. But if this region had one-tenth of a Christian population at the end of the second century, the proportion must have been vastly greater by the end of the third century, after the long period of peace, during which, as we know from Eusebius,[2] the Church was progressing by "leaps and bounds."

Churches in Germany, Spain, Gaul, in the East, in Egypt, in Libya, &c., as agreeing in the symbol of the faith (*Adv. Hær.* i. 7).

[1] *Untergang*, p. 4.   [2] VIII. 1.

This is borne out by the glimpses we get of the affluence of the Church in the times of Cyprian and Constantine; by the very magnitude and importance of its schisms— notably the Donatist; and by the extraordinary number of its bishops.[1]

The situation was not widely different in Alexandria. From the appearance of the developed Gnosticism of Basilides and Valentinus in the early part of the century, we know that Christianity must early have taken hold upon this famous city—as motley in its habits of thought as in its population; and we have an incidental corroboration of this in a curious letter of the versatile Emperor Hadrian, whose satiric strain throws an interesting light on the strangely mixed state of affairs which prevailed. " I have

[1] In the year 330 the Donatists alone could bring together a Synod of 270 bishops. See further on the Church of Carthage in Lect. II.

found the people," he says, "vain, fickle, and shifting, with every breath of opinion. Those who worship Serapis are in fact Christians, and they who call themselves Christian bishops are actually worshippers of Serapis. . . . The patriarch himself, when he comes to Egypt, is compelled by one party to worship Serapis, by the other Christ."[1] Here is already a very marked diffusion of Christianity in Alexandria in the first quarter of the second century, and a corresponding interest of the emperors in it. While naming Hadrian, I may simply quote for what it is worth the remarkable statement made regarding him by the heathen writer Lampridius, viz., that he at one time contemplated dedicating to Christ statues without temples which he had caused to be erected in every city, and was only deterred by the consideration " that

[1] Letter to Servianus. See text in Lightfoot, *Ignatius*, I. p. 464.

the temples of the old gods would become deserted, and all the people would become Christian" (*omnes Christianos futuros*).[1] Even if erroneous, the statement is a striking testimony to the impression which Christianity must have produced on the Hadrianic age.

The position of the Church in Alexandria was greatly strengthened by the rise of its famous Catechetical School. It is right, however, that I should say a word at this point on the testimony of Origen, who, from Gibbon downwards, has been cited as a counter-witness that the number of Christians in his days were " very few." It would be strange indeed if Origen, in the middle of the third century, should make any such assertion, and we shall find, I think, that it is forcing his language to put this interpreta-

[1] Lamprid. in *Sev. Alex.*, 43; cf. Lightfoot, *Ignatius*, I. p. 441; Lanciani, *Pag. and Christ. Rome*, p. 11.

EARLY PROGRESS OF CHRISTIANITY 69

tion upon it. The passage in question is in the eighth book against Celsus, where Origen is urging the blessing that would accrue to the Roman Empire if men universally acted on the spirit of Christ's precept, " If two of you shall agree on earth as touching anything that they shall ask," &c. " What might we expect," he says, " if not only a very few (πάνυ ὀλίγοι) agree, as at present, but the whole of the Empire of Rome?"[1] It is plainly unfair, especially in view of Origen's own declarations elsewhere,[2] to

[1] Origen, *Contra Celsum*, viii. 69.

[2] In bk. viii. 14, *e.g.*, Origen speaks of the "multitude" of believers in the Church. He cites Celsus (iii. 10) to the effect that when the Christians were few in number they held the same opinion, but when they became "a great multitude" they were divided and separated ; and he says " That Christians at first were few in number is undoubted, in comparison with the multitudes who subsequently became Christians ; and yet, all things considered, they were not (even then) so very few." (Cf. iii. 9, 29, and see below.) Of course the numerical inferiority of the Christians to the Pagans was still striking, even if

strain a passage like this, which relates to agreement in prayer, into a statistical declaration of the number of Christians in the Empire. Remembering the distinction between real and nominal Christianity, we might say with some justice that even in Britain and America at the present day "very few" agree. The truth is that Origen is one of the most explicit witnesses we possess to the victorious progress which Christianity was making in the Empire. In that very eighth book to which reference is made, and in the same context, he expresses his triumphant confidence, despite of oppression and persecution, that Christianity is the power destined to overcome every other. " Every form of worship," he says, "will be destroyed except the religion of Christ, which will alone prevail. And indeed it will one

the former composed one-fourth or one-fifth of the population of the cities.

EARLY PROGRESS OF CHRISTIANITY 71

day triumph, as its principles take possession of the minds of men more and more every day."[1] And repeatedly in the course of his work he bears witness to the all-conquering power of the truth. "It proved victorious," he says, "as being the word of God, the very nature of which is such that it cannot be hindered; and becoming more powerful than all such adversaries, it made itself master of the whole of Greece and a considerable portion of barbarian lands, and converted countless numbers (myriads) to his religion."[2] This is a considerably different picture from

[1] Bk. viii. 68. This, it has been remarked, is a new idea, remarkably opposed to the tone of the earlier writers, who always look on the Roman power as hostile and persecuting, an oppression from which there could be no deliverance except through the coming of the end.

[2] Bk. i. 27; cf. ii. 13: "For the Word, spoken with power, has gained the mastery over men of all sorts of nature, and it is impossible to see any race of men which has escaped accepting the teaching of Jesus"; and iii. 24: "He (Celsus) cannot

the " very few," to which we are wont to be referred as Origen's sole testimony! The most convincing evidence, perhaps, of the enormous progress the gospel must have made in Alexandria and similar great cities by the time of Constantine is the way in which, after the victory of Christianity, the conflicts of Christians and Pagans seem to sink into the background, while the stage is filled with new disputants, Catholic and Donatist, Orthodox and Arian, in whose disputes the very heathen take their share, ridiculing them in the theatres, and discussing them in the baths, shops, and streets.[1]

demonstrate that an unspeakable number, as he asserts, of Greeks and Barbarians acknowledge the existence of Æsculapius ; while we, if we deem this a matter of importance, can clearly show a countless multitude of Greeks and Barbarians who acknowledge the existence of Jesus." (Also vii. 26.)

[1] Cf. *Histories* of Socrates (i. 6, 8 ; ii. 2) ; Theod., (i. 6), &c. See passages collected in Newman's *Arians*, Note V.

Yet in this great and populous city—the second in the Empire—Schultze will only grant a minimum of some 50,000 Christians, or one-twelfth of its 600,000 inhabitants.[1] Surely, again, an immense understatement!

From Carthage and Alexandria our eyes turn to a third great centre—Antioch, the gay and voluptuous capital of Syria, which, in point of population and influence, stood only behind Alexandria. Apart from the list of its bishops and other slight notices in Eusebius,[2] the Church of this city, renowned in the earliest age as the Mother Church of Gentile Christianity, is another of those that only come late into view. When it does

[1] Pp. 20-1. He allows 150,000 for Egypt and Libya. On the opulence of the Alexandrian Church, see next lecture.

[2] These, however, suffice to show an important Church. The Epistles of Ignatius alone are evidence of this.

become distinctly visible in the middle of the third century, it is as a seat of ecclesiastical influence of the first rank. The extraordinary splendour of its episcopate, and elaboration of its Church service, under the notorious Paul of Samosata [1]; its influential councils and important theological school; the magnificent Golden Church reared later by the liberality of Constantine [2]; its prominence in the Arian controversies; the utter failure of Julian's attempt to restore Paganism in it—readers of Church History will remember his chagrin when, having gone to celebrate with all pomp the festival of Apollo at the Temple of Daphne, he found only a single old priest, sacrificing a goose at his own expense [3]; the flourishing

[1] Cf. Eus. vii. 30.

[2] Eus., *Life of Constantine*, iii. 50; Orat. 9. "A church of unparalleled size and beauty." Its dedication in A.D. 341 was the occasion of a Council famous in the Arian strife.

[3] Julian himself relates the incident in his *Misopogon*.

state of the Church, numerically at least, under Chrysostom—all this shows that, even before the change of the political relations, Christianity must have been practically in the ascendant in the city. " Probably already (in first half of fourth century)," says V. Schultze, "at all events soon after, the majority and power were in the possession of the Christians."[1] We have the express testimony of Chrysostom that in his day the Christians were a majority in the city (τὸ πλέον τῆς πόλεως χριστιανικόν)[2]; and this is borne out by the separate figures he gives, showing the population to have been 200,000,[3] and the number of the Christian community about 100,000.[4] But even these figures pro-

[1] *Untergang*, II. p. 261.   [2] *Adv. Jud. hom.*, i. 4.
[3] *Hom. in St. Ignat.*, 4.
[4] *Hom. in Matt.*, lxxxv. (lxxxvi.) 4. On the debatable elements in these figures, see Gibbon, ch. xv., and V. Schultze, II. p. 263. These writers suppose that Chrysostom reckons only citizens of Antioch—*i.e.*,

bably do not do justice to the strength of Christianity in the Syrian capital. In a vast city like Antioch, as in other great centres, there must have been a large floating mass favourably disposed to Christianity, who yet never definitely connected themselves with the Church. What it is still more important to remember, Antioch at this time was a city deeply rent with schisms. There were, in fact, in Chrysostom's day, no fewer than three rival parties in it, two at least with separate organisations, all holding ecclesiastically aloof from each other—the Catholic, the Arian, and the Meletian.[1] It is an interesting question whether in his 100,000

not children or slaves—and Gibbon would raise the number of inhabitants to half a million. Be that as it may, Chrysostom's statements, which V. Schultze accepts, as to the relative proportions, are not to be set aside.

[1] "The unhappy Church" was thus, as Mr. Stephens says, "torn to tatters" (*Saint Chrysostom*, pp. 21, 140).

EARLY PROGRESS OF CHRISTIANITY 77

Christians he reckoned, as his language would seem to imply,[1] only the frequenters of his own cathedral, or the schismatics as well. In any case, we have his explicit statement that the Christian community in Antioch outnumbered the Jews and Pagans combined ; and this reflects light back on the prosperous condition of the Church in the beginning of the century. It is a natural but hasty assumption that the mere change in imperial favour constituted a reason why, in such a city, those who had been previously Pagan should at once rush into the arms of the Church. Imperial favour would no doubt have its effect, but the city did not change its creed at the bidding of Julian, and there is no reason to suppose it would have become

[1] He speaks of "those assembling there" (τοὺς ἐνταῦθα συναγομένους), *i.e.*, at the church. This is to be borne in mind, if it should be the case (see above), that the 200,000 in Antioch only represent the citizen element in the population.

Christian at the bidding of Constantine had the public mind not otherwise been prepared to receive the new faith.

The case of Antioch just cited has a bearing on our subject in another way; has, in fact, been used by Gibbon for the directly opposite purpose of establishing his low estimate of the numbers of Christians in Rome and in the Empire. Unwarrantably, as I think, in face of Chrysostom's statements, reckoning the Christians in Antioch at one-fifth, instead of one-half, of the population, he makes this the basis of a calculation to show that the proportion elsewhere is, as he represents it, one-twentieth of the whole.[1] Two sets of data are combined in his argument—one, a notice in Chrysostom that in Antioch 3,000 widows and virgins were supported by the bounty of the Church[2]; and the other, a statement in Eusebius that in the year 250

[1] Ch. xv.   [2] *Hom. in Matt.* lxvi. (lxvii.) 3.

EARLY PROGRESS OF CHRISTIANITY 79

A.D., the clergy of Rome consisted of a bishop, 46 presbyters, 7 deacons, as many subdeacons, with 42 acolytes, and 52 readers, exorcists, and porters, while the number of widows and poor supported by the Church was over 1,500.[1] This small number of the clergy, and the fact that the numbers supported by charity are half those in Antioch, with its Church community of 100,000, are held to justify the inference that the Church in Rome must have had about 50,000 members. But it must surely be felt that we are on very precarious ground indeed in reasoning from a bare enumeration of the clergy and poor to the strength of the Christian community in Rome, especially when Cornelius, the author of the above enumeration, in the same breath speaks of "the very great, even innumerable people" (μεγίστου καὶ ἀναριθμήτου λαοῦ) whom these clergy served! We

[1] *Ecc. Hist.* vi. 43.

know far too little of the ecclesiastical arrangements of the Roman Church—of the number of its parishes, and of the manner in which the work of these parishes was overtaken by the clergy,[1] to be able to hazard even a guess at the ratio of the clergy to the body of the people. In Antioch itself, where the Christians were at least 100,000 strong, we have no hint of a division into districts with separate churches at all; the preaching, so far as would appear, was done, chiefly by Chrysostom, at the one great cathedral.[2] The great church at Constantinople, again, in the time of Justinian, when practically all were

[1] We have the testimony of Optatus of Mileve that there were forty churches in Rome before the last persecution. Cf. *Bingham*, III. p. 133. But we have only to reflect on the number of parochial churches in some of our large continental cities still—a dozen or little more to an immense population—to see that this is no index to the numbers of the Christian following.

[2] Mr. Stephen points this out in his *Saint Chrysostom*, p. 108.

nominally Christian, was served, as we learn from Gibbon himself,[1] by but sixty presbyters. It is at least equally precarious to reason from the numbers of widows and poor in one community to those in another, without knowing the precise circumstances of each and their respective modes of administering help. But apart from all other considerations, the Catacomb discoveries already adverted to seem to demonstrate the baselessness of Gibbon's calculations.

Our materials are scantier, when from these large and flourishing churches of the East, we turn to the West, and inquire concerning the progress of the gospel in Gaul and Spain. The origin of the Church in Gaul is wrapped in obscurity, and we need not seek to penetrate the mists of legend which enshroud it. The first real glimpse we get of it is in the beautiful and pathetic narrative of

[1] Ch. xx., footnote to No. 2, on Clergy.

the martyrdoms at Vienne and Lyons, under Marcus Aurelius, in the year 177 A.D.[1] We have only to think, however, of what that single glimpse reveals, to be satisfied that the Kingdom of Heaven, which is like leaven, was silently and secretly diffusing itself in Gaul, as everywhere else. Dean Milman speaks too sanguinely, perhaps, when he says of this reign of Marcus, "The western provinces, Gaul and Africa, rivalled the East in the number, if not in the opulence of their Christian congregations. In almost every city had gradually arisen a separate community,"[2] but we may safely conclude that our temptation is to minimise, rather than to magnify, what had actually been accomplished. The Church at Lyons, at the head of which Irenæus now takes his place as bishop, shows how Christianity had established itself at a point of

[1] Eus. v. 1., 2.   [2] *Hist. of Christ.*, bk. ii. ch. 7.

vantage, the value of which, for purposes of aggression, can hardly be over-estimated. Only when, with the aid of a description like Renan's,[1] we picture to ourselves the superlative importance of Lyons as a political religious, and commercial centre, and realise its geographical advantage as situated at the junction of the Rhone and the Saône, do we appreciate how much was secured by the gospel having attained, even at the cost of fearful sufferings, a firm footing in its midst. Neither does it follow that, because Christianity was late in taking root in Gaul, its progress, once it had established itself, was not as rapid there as elsewhere.[2] Unfortunately, our means of information are so slight that we are unable to trace its advances in detail. We have a rhetorical

[1] *Marc-Aurèle*, ch. xix. Cf. Schultze, *Untergang*, II. pp. 110–12 : "The capital of the Three Gauls."

[2] The culture conditions were exceptionally favourable. Cf. Schultze, II. p. 101.

84 NEGLECTED FACTORS IN THE

allusion in Tertullian [1]; we glean scattered hints of congregations in the third century; we find Constantius and Constantine protecting the Christians in Gaul in the Diocletian persecution [2]; we have the important Synod in Arles in 314 A.D., another Church coming suddenly into view [3]; we have notices thus early of numerous bishoprics [4]; while by the middle of the fourth century we find an episcopal organisation in all the provinces of the country.[5] But the best proof of all of the rapid march of the gospel to victory is the fact which Schultze emphasises, of the complete overthrow of the classical Paganism in the cities throughout all Gaul in the course of

[1] *Adv. Jud.* 7.

[2] Eus., *Life of Constantine*, i. 8, 15, 16, &c.

[3] Cf. Hefele, II. pp. 180 ff. (E. T.) "The Synod of Arles," says Schultze, "shows that Christianity had gone deep into the community" (II. p. 13).

[4] Schultze, *Untergang*, I. p. 12.

[5] Ibid. II. p. 103.

the fourth century.[1] How this victory was brought about we can only imperfectly discern in the labours of such outstanding individuals as Hilary of Poitiers and Martin of Tours, but the decisiveness and completeness of the transition is as remarkable as anything in history.

If, in this paucity of evidence, it be thought that we assume too much in supposing a silent but steady progress of the gospel through Gaul in the third century, an apt instance to rebuke our scepticism comes from the neighbouring Church of Spain. The early history of the Church in Spain is even more completely hidden from us than that of the Church in Gaul. The sum-

[1] *Untergang*, II. pp. 103, 113-14, &c. The Celtic heathenism lingered longer, though also in the main overcome. Mommsen (quoted by Schultze, II. p. 116) says, " More rapidly still than the (Celtic) native speech, the native religion lost ground, and Christianity, pressing in, found in it scarcely any opposition."

total of our knowledge of it during the first three centuries is comprised in casual allusions in Irenæus and Tertullian,[1] and in an Epistle of Cyprian which relates to the deposition of two Spanish bishops.[2] The curtain lifts, as usual suddenly, at the Council of Elvira, A.D. 305 or 306—a Council whose 81 Canons still remain to us.[3] And what do we find then? A Church long rooted in the land, with splendid basilicas, reckoning in its membership great landowners, and numerous magistrates, and high civic dignitaries, while an eagerness is shown on the part of all sections of the community—including those whose occupations are most questionable—

[1] Iren. i. 10; Tert. *Adv. Jud.* 7.

[2] Epistle 67. The Epistle is, however, of importance as showing the sufferings of the Spanish Church in the Decian Persecution.

[3] See in Hefele, I. pp. 180 ff. The Council of Elvira, with its 19 bishops and 24 presbyters, is only to be regarded as representing the South of Spain. Cf. Schultze, I. p. 5.

to be received into its communion. Hosius, the Bishop of Cordova, was the trusted adviser of Constantine, and a leading figure in the Nicene Council.

This brings us to the final struggle—the persecution inaugurated by Diocletian—from the midst of which come some remarkable testimonies, with the mention of which I may fitly conclude this portion of the argument. The Church had been at peace for forty years, and its progress during that period had been extraordinarily rapid. "Who could describe," says Eusebius, "those vast collections of men that flocked to the religion of Christ, and those multitudes crowding in from every city, and the illustrious concourse in the houses of worship?"[1] Then the persecution burst, sifting the ranks of the Church, and scattering nominal professors before it, as a storm breaking through a forest makes the

[1] *Ecc. Hist.*, viii. 1 ; Cf. Lect. III.

leaves fly in every direction. The incidents of the persecution — which we do not stay to describe—and other notices of the time, show how widely Christianity must have been spread. We read, for example, of a town in Phrygia burned with all its population, including women and children, because the inhabitants, those in high rank as well as persons of humbler station, confessed themselves Christians, and would not recant![1] We should notice also the case of Armenia, which at this time received the gospel from Gregory the Illuminator, and that so decidedly that probably two-thirds of the people may be reckoned as professing Christianity.[2] Incidentally, we get a glimpse of the predominance of Christianity in Rome in the fact, narrated by Eusebius, that Maxentius, the usurper of imperial power in Italy during the persecution, sought

[1] *Ecc. Hist.*, viii. 11. [2] Cf. Schultze, I. p. 17.

to ingratiate himself with the Romans by pretending that he was of the Christian faith. "He pretended," says the historian, "by a species of accommodation and flattery towards the Romans, that he was of our faith."[1] But there are yet more striking testimonies. The complete failure of the persecution may be said to be itself such a testimony, as, indeed, the persecutors themselves, in their edicts and rescripts of toleration, acknowledge.[2] Maximin, Emperor of the East, was the most obstinate and cruel, perhaps, of all these persecutors. And what does he say? In an Epistle to his governors ordering the persecution to cease, he gives as the reason why it had been undertaken actually this—*that the emperors "had seen that almost all men* (σχεδὸν ἅπαντας ἀνθρώπους) *were abandoning the worship of the gods, and attaching themselves to the party*

[1] Eus. viii. 14.   [2] Ibid. viii. 16, 17; ix. 9.

(ἔθνει) *of the Christians.*"[1] Rhetoric may be charged against Tertullian, but a proclamation of this kind is hardly one in which we should look for rhetorical exaggeration! The only other testimony I shall adduce is one from the Christian side. It is that of the famous Lucian of Antioch, teacher of Arius, and founder of the school usually known as the Antiochian, who perished in the persecution. And the words of Lucian are that, prior to the last persecution, "*almost the greater part of the world, including whole cities, had yielded obedience to the truth*" ("pars paene mundi jam major huic veritati adstipulatur ; urbes integræ ").[2] These are utterances from the midst of

[1] Eus. ix. 9.

[2] The passage is only in the Latin translation of Eusebius by Rufinus, but Dr. Milman thinks it authentic; cf. *Hist. of Christ.*, Bk. iii., ch. i. He quotes also a note from Routh, who gives on the authority of Porson a statement from Porphyry, that the Christians were τοὺς πλείονας—a majority.

the conflict, not easily to be explained away by those who would persuade us that the Christians constituted only an insignificant one-twentieth, or even one-tenth of the population, at the time of the victory ; and they surely warrant us in holding that there has been an undue timidity in recognising the powerful hold which Christianity had taken, numerically, on society by the end of the third century. If we allow the simple facts of the case to produce their natural impression on our minds our verdict, I think, must be—there are factors here which have been neglected.

THE EXTENSION OF CHRISTIANITY *VERTICALLY*, OR AS RESPECTS THE DIFFERENT STRATA OF SOCIETY.

Influence of Christianity on the higher ranks of society under-estimated—New Testament evidence—Witness of the Catacombs—Pomponia Græcina—Flavius Clemens and Domitilla—Acilius Glabrio—Notices in Second Century—The wealth of the Church of Rome—The witness of the persecutions—Tertullian and Clement on luxury of Christians—Relations of Christianity with the Imperial Court in the Third Century—The Decian persecution and its effects—The Church before and under Diocletian—Social status of Church teachers—Result : membership of the Early Church not drawn mainly from the lowest, but from the intermediate classes, and embraced many of the wealthier and higher orders.

LECTURE II

THE EXTENSION OF CHRISTIANITY *VERTI-CALLY*, OR AS RESPECTS THE DIFFERENT STRATA OF SOCIETY

IN the previous lecture I defended the position that Christianity in the early centuries had manifested an energy of propagation, and diffused itself with a rapidity much greater than the majority of Church historians seem prepared to allow; I am now to seek to strengthen this position by taking society, as it were, in vertical section, and inquiring into the degree in which Christianity can be shown to have affected the wealthier and better-educated classes in the Empire, as well as those of inferior social station. Here also, I think, the influence of the gospel has generally been under-estimated. It may be going too far to say, with Prof. Ramsay, that Christianity "spread at first among the educated more rapidly than among the uneducated"[1]; but I am persuaded that even this is nearer the truth than the opinion often expressed that Christianity drew the great bulk of its adherents in the earliest times from persons of the lowest and most servile positions—that, in Gibbon's well-known words, the new sect was "almost entirely composed of the dregs of the populace—of peasants and mechanics, of boys and women, of beggars and slaves."[2] To say that Christianity began with the

[1] *Church in Roman Empire*, p. 57.

[2] Gibbon gives this as "the charge of malice and infidelity," which he proceeds in part to qualify.

EARLY PROGRESS OF CHRISTIANITY 97

lowest classes, and gradually worked up to the higher, is at best a half-truth. It is not less true that the gospel often laid hold first of persons in better social position, and from them worked around and down. Its Divine power drew to it men of all classes of society from the beginning, and often the persons in higher station were the first to come, and, through their example, brought others. The evidence on this, as on the other branches of our subject, has been gradually accumulating, and in recent years has come to be much better appreciated. Still, as respects the ordinary treatment of Church History, it may justly be said that not a little of it is " a neglected factor."

In supporting this thesis, which will seem to many paradoxical, I do not wish to be misunderstood. It is not disputed that in the days of the Apostles, and so long as Christianity was a proscribed religion, the numbers of the wealthy, and learned, and powerful, belonging to it were still comparatively few, and that the body of the membership of the Church consisted of persons of the humbler and middle ranks of society.[1] The wealthy and noble must *always* be few in comparison with others in the Church, for this, if for no other reason, that there are fewer of them. This is Origen's reply to Celsus as respects the intelligence of the Christians, that " among the multitude of converts to Christianity, the simple and ignorant necessarily outnumbered the more intelligent, as *the former class always does the latter*." [2] Even yet the greater part of our

[1] The rude, misspelt scrawls and execrable Latinity of many of the Catacomb inscriptions are sufficient evidence of this. The contrast has often been drawn between the finely executed Pagan epitaphs on one side of the Lapidarian Gallery in the Vatican, and the hasty, illiterate scribbles of the Catacomb series opposite. (Cf. Hasenclever in *Jahr. f. Prot. Theol.*, VIII. pp. 34–5.) [2] *Contra Celsum*, i. 27.

Christian congregations does not consist of nobles and millionaires, but of persons drawn from the intermediate and humbler classes of society — tradespeople, artisans, peasants, and the *best* part of these — and still more must this have been the case when there was far less of a middle class than there is now,[1] and trade and industry were left chiefly in the hands of freedmen, foreigners, and slaves. But this inferior social rank of the earlier converts to Christianity has been greatly exaggerated. The sneer of Celsus[2] which Origen refutes has been repeated as if it were a true description of Christian society, instead of a caricature. We shall see that if, as Paul says, "not many wise after the flesh, not many mighty, not many noble" were called,[3] there were still, all

[1] Some would say no middle class at all, but this is an exaggeration. Cf. the sentence from Schultze, on p. 112.

[2] *Contra Celsum*, iii. 55.   [3] 1 Cor. i. 26.

things considered, a surprising number from these very classes and from the intermediate ranks—and as time went on still more—who adorned by their faith the doctrine of God their Saviour. I am far, indeed, from suggesting that Christianity derives a lustre from the mere social rank of its converts, which would not be lent to it by the virtues of the humblest.[1] The flow of rank and wealth into the Church, far from proving a source of blessing to it, has proved often a cause of backsliding and corruption. But it may fairly be contended that just in proportion to the obstacles which lay in the way of persons of rank and wealth becoming members of an obscure and uninfluential sect, the more signally was the power of the gospel magnified in overcoming these obstacles, and bringing them to the feet of the Crucified. Neither must we under-esti-

[1] Cf. James ii. 5.

mate the effects on the progress of Christianity of the influence and example of persons of this class. That influence was great, and in the providential order had much to do with the commending of the gospel in the circles in which it operated.

An instructive fore-glimpse of what is afterwards to be illustrated in the history of the Church is already furnished in the personal ministry of its Founder. The wealthy and official classes, we know, as a body rejected Christ, while "the common people heard Him gladly."[1] The question could be asked, "Have any of the rulers believed on Him, or of the Pharisees?"[2] Yet if we look a little more carefully into the list of Christ's personal disciples and followers, we shall find, I think, that they are drawn neither from the highest, nor

[1] Mark xii. 37.   [2] John vii. 48.

preponderatingly from the lowest, ranks of society, but from what we should now call the middle classes; while instances are not wanting to show the power of the gospel on persons of higher social position. Thus, among the friends and followers of Jesus we have mention made of certain women who had been healed by Him and attended Him, including—with Mary Magdalene— "Joanna, the wife of Chuza, Herod's steward, and Susanna, and many others, who ministered to Him of their substance"[1]; we have the family of Bethany—Lazarus and his sisters—evidently of good social position; we have, in the band of the Apostles, the pairs of brothers, Simon and Andrew, and James and John, who, though fishermen, were at least in comfortable circumstances—Zebedee with his sons owning boats and hired servants, and carrying on a fishery business in

[1] Luke viii. 2.

EARLY PROGRESS OF CHRISTIANITY 103

partnership with Simon [1]; we have the publicans, Matthew and Zacchæus, the one able to make "a great feast in his house" on occasion of his Call,[2] the other "a chief publican," and "rich"[3]; we have the Roman centurion, who had built the Jews a synagogue —no mean personage therefore [4]—and Jairus, one of the rulers of the synagogue [5]; we have Nicodemus, a ruler of the Jews, and Joseph of Arimathea, "a councillor of honourable estate," and "rich"[6]; we have the testimony in John, "Nevertheless even of the rulers many believed on Him, but because of the Pharisees, they did not confess it"[7]; we have such instances as that of the rich young

---

[1] Mark i. 20; Luke v. 10. Nathanael (= Bartholomew?) also seems to have been a man of good social standing (Cf. John i. 45–51). It is noticeable that members of this group are found at a distance from their homes in Judea, waiting as disciples on the Baptist (John i.). [2] Luke v. 29.
[3] Ibid. xix. 2. [4] Ibid. vii. 5. [5] Mark v. 22.
[6] Mark xv. 43; Matt. xxvii. 57. [7] John xii. 42.

ruler attracted to Christ,[1] of the candid scribe who was "not far from the kingdom of God,"[2] of the other scribe who impulsively offered his service.[3] All this, when, to use the words of the Evangelist, "the Spirit was not yet given, because Jesus was not yet glorified."[4]

Passing from the Gospels to the Church in the Apostolic age, we have a new series of examples which look in the same direction. The mother church at Jerusalem had among its members possessors of lands and houses, apparently not a few, who sold them and laid the proceeds, in whole or part, at the Apostles' feet.[5] We have specific instances in Barnabas of Cyprus, who, having land, sold it[6]; in Ananias and Sapphira, who sold a possession and deceitfully kept back part of the price[7]; in the mother of

[1] Luke xviii. 18, 23. [2] Mark xii. 34.
[3] Matt. viii. 19. [4] John vii. 39. [5] Acts iv. 34, 35.
[6] Ibid. iv. 37. [7] Ibid. v. 1, 2.

John Mark, who had a house of her own in Jerusalem.[1] Many of the converts at Pentecost were persons who had come long and expensive journeys to the feast [2]; and at an early stage in the history it is testified, "A great company of the priests were obedient to the faith."[3] The eighth chapter of the Acts records how the eunuch of Ethiopia, described as "of great authority under Candace, queen of the Ethiopians, who was over all her treasure,"[4] was brought to faith by the Evangelist Philip; the ninth chapter relates the conversion of the great Apostle of the Gentiles, Saul of Tarsus, pupil of Gamaliel, who, as a Roman citizen, may be assumed to have been of a good family [5]; the eleventh chapter tells of Peter's successful mission to the devout centurion Cornelius—a man noted for his

[1] Acts xii. 12.   [2] Ibid. ii. 5.
[3] Ibid. vi. 7.   [4] Ibid. viii. 27.
[5] Cf. Ramsay's *St. Paul the Traveller*, ch. ii.

alms.[1] A new beginning in the Christian propaganda is made in the Gentile Church at Antioch, and here, among the prophets and teachers who designate Saul and Barnabas to their work, we find Manaen, the foster-brother of Herod the Tetrarch.[2] Following the Apostle in his missionary journeyings, we have continual examples of how the word took root in the hearts of persons of the higher ranks, even more readily, often, than in the minds of the multitude. Thus the visit to Cyprus issued in the confusion of Elymas the Magian and the conversion of the Proconsul Sergius Paulus.[3] The first convert in Philippi was Lydia, the well-to-do seller of purple.[4] In Thessalonica a great multitude of devout Greeks (proselytes) believed, and it is expressly recorded, "of the chief women not

[1] Acts x. 2, 31.   [2] Ibid. xiii. 1.
[3] Ibid. xiii. 12.   [4] Ibid. xvi. 14.

EARLY PROGRESS OF CHRISTIANITY 107

a few."[1] Jason, who received the preachers into his house and shielded them from violence, was evidently a man of substance.[2] In the neighbouring city of Berœa it is attested that many believed, "also of the Greek women of honourable estate, and of men, not a few."[3] Athens gave but few converts, but one of them was Dionysius the Areopagite.[4] There is nothing in all this of the gospel working its way gradually up from below. It goes straight to the hearts of these people of honourable estate from the lips of the preacher, or from the Scriptures "searched daily."[5] At Corinth, besides the tent-makers Aquila and Priscilla, who cannot be described as poor, we have Crispus, the chief ruler of the synagogue, "believing in the Lord with all his house"[6];

[1] Acts xvii. 4.   [2] Ibid. xvii. 9.
[3] Ibid. xvii. 12.   [4] Ibid. xvii. 34.
   Ibid. xvii. 11.   [6] Ibid. xviii. 8.

at Ephesus we have the conversion of the dealers in magic arts and the burning of the great pile of their books of sorcery [1]; at the island of Malta we have the cure—if not the conversion—of the governor Publius,[2] with many other indications of a similar kind. Moving through the history of the "Acts," in fact, and gleaning the impressions which its pictures of the life and work and trials of these early Christian brotherhoods make upon us, we never feel ourselves in contact with Gibbon's "dregs of the populace," but are consciously at every point in touch with intelligent, well-ordered, and socially reputable communities. These notices in the Book of Acts receive confirmation and amplification from the Epistles, if there also, in many of the Churches, darker shades appear. The Church at Corinth, to which Paul wrote that "not many

Acts xix. 19.   [2] Ibid. xxviii. 8.

EARLY PROGRESS OF CHRISTIANITY 109

wise, not many mighty, not many noble" are called, embraced in its membership, besides Crispus, the chief ruler of the synagogue, Erastus, the chamberlain of the city [1]; while the disorders at the Agape and many other indications — the taste of the Church, for instance, for rhetoric and Alexandrian wisdom, its conceit of knowledge, its lawsuits of the brethren one with another,[2] its heresies on the resurrection — show that it was not a church composed exclusively, or even predominatingly, of the poorer classes, but a church, rather, intellectually disposed, and containing in it a good many people of better social position. To this church belonged the much-praised "household of Stephanas."[3] I need only allude—for I cannot delay long on this part of the subject—to such other characters in the Epistles as Philemon of

[1] Rom. xvi. 23.   [2] 1 Cor. vi. 6.   [3] Ibid. xvi. 15.

Colosse, the master of Onesimus,[1] the hospitable Onesiphorus,[2] the well-beloved Gaius,[3] and the most excellent Theophilus, to whom the Evangelist Luke,[4] himself a physician,[5] writes his "treatises." The Epistles bear witness in our favour in other and less direct ways. If the Apostolic Churches had slaves in their membership, they had also masters, to whom exhortations are addressed.[6] Specially instructive in this connection are the passages directed against the dangers and abuses of wealth, as, *e.g.*, where Paul exhorts, "Charge them that are rich in this present world, that they be not high-minded, nor have their hope set on the uncertainty of riches, but on God"[7]; or where James cautions against partiality to the man with the gold ring and fine

---

[1] Ep. to Phil. [2] 2 Tim. i. 16.
[3] 3 John. [4] Luke i. 3 ; Acts i. 1.
[5] Col. iv. 14. [6] Eph. vi. 9 ; Col. iv. 1.
[7] 1 Tim. vi. 17 ; cf. vers. 9, 10.

clothing, and denounces the rich men who rob the labourers of their hire.[1] Finally, we have the picture of the Church of Laodicea in the Book of Revelation, which boasts of being rich and increased with goods—if this is to be taken literally—and is all the while in deep spiritual poverty.[2] We have, on the other hand, the testimony of the Apostle to "the deep poverty" of the Churches of Macedonia—connected, however, with a special season of tribulation—but also his witness to their abundant liberality in the collection made for the poor saints in Judea.[3] I do not think it is an unreasonable conclusion to draw from these data that, while there were doubtless poor churches, and many poor people in all the churches, the general membership of the congregations

[1] James ii. 2, 5 ; v. 4. The latter passage need not refer to Christians.
[2] Rev. iii. 17.   [3] 2 Cor. viii. 2 ; ix.

was, contrary to the usual view, composed of fairly well-to-do and intelligent people and commonly had among them also persons of highly respectable, and sometimes quite conspicuous positions. I am glad in this view to find myself supported by the writer already frequently quoted—V. Schultze. "It was not the base elements," he says, "which came into the Church; but, on the contrary, the better strata of the Roman population, the artificers, the shopkeepers, and the small landed proprietors, therefore preponderatingly the under and middle portion of the citizen class, who, in the general moral and religious dissolution of heathenism, still proved themselves the soundest classes in the community."[1] I

[1] *Untergang*, I. p. 25. I may quote here also Dean Merivale's judgment. "I have shown in another place," he says, "that the gospel was not embraced, on its first promulgation in Judea, by the despair of the most wretched outcasts of humanity, but rather

EARLY PROGRESS OF CHRISTIANITY 113

propose, in the remainder of the lecture, to adduce some of the evidence furnished by early ecclesiastical history, which, I think, makes clear the justice of this contention.

Here, again, I can have no hesitation in placing in the forefront of my argument the comparatively recent and singularly impressive testimony of the Catacombs. The evidence which has come to us from this quarter is partly elucidatory and corroborative of what had formerly been conjectured; but

by the hopeful enthusiasm which urges those enjoying a portion of the goods of life to improve and fortify their position. And so again at Rome we have no reason to suppose that Christianity was only the refuge of the afflicted and miserable; rather, if we may lay any stress on the monuments above referred to, it was first embraced by persons in a certain grade of comfort and respectability; by persons approaching to what we should call *the middle classes* in their condition, their education, and their moral views."—*The Romans under the Empire,* ch. liv. See further Dean Milman's judgment cited below, p. 142.

much of it, also, is entirely new, and to it chiefly, perhaps, is due the revived interest which of late years has been shown in this subject of the social rank of the early Christians. The very existence of these Catacombs, it may be remarked at the outset, taken in connection with the circumstances of their origin, is a proof that the Church of Rome must from the earliest period have had among its members persons of wealth and distinction. The oldest of the Catacombs go back to the first century—one or two perhaps to Apostolic days. In nearly all cases they seem to have been begun as private burial-places in the gardens or vineyards of persons of the wealthier class,[1] while the elegance and refinement of their construction, and the elaboration of their decorations, point to lavish outlay by their owners.[2]

[1] Cf. Northcote and Brownlow, I. pp. 101, 114 ff.
[2] This artistic elegance and finish is characteristic

In some cases spots of ground were directly gifted to the Church for the burial of the brethren.[1] But it is chiefly in the inscriptions, enabling us positively to identify particular crypts with individuals and families, that the interest of this class of discoveries culminates. ¶The amount of light thrown in this way on the extent to which Christianity had penetrated into the higher Roman circles is really very surprising. I shall notice a few of the best known cases, combining with the light furnished by the Catacombs such knowledge of the facts as comes to us from other sources.

An early case of great interest is that of Pomponia Græcina in the reign of Nero. The New Testament acquaints us with the fact

of all the cemeteries which on other grounds are shown to go back to first century. Cf. Northcote and Brownlow, as above; *Dict. of Christ. Antiq.*, I. p. 303.

[1] Cf. Lanciani, *Pagan and Christ. Rome*, p. 336.

that Christianity had early obtained a footing in that immense establishment known as "Cæsar's Household."[1] Prof. Ramsay quotes from Mommsen the observation that nowhere had Christianity a stronger hold than in the household and at the court of the Emperors.[2] But that, beyond this household, Christianity had found its way into the highest circles, had long been

[1] Phil. iv. 22. See the description of this gigantic establishment in Lightfoot's *Philippians*, pp. 171 ff ; also Friedländer, *Sittengeschichte Roms*, I. pp. 71–210. Withrow states : |" In remarkable confirmation of this fact is the discovery in the recent explorations of the ruins of the Imperial Palace [Nero's " Golden House "], of several Christian memorials, including one of those lamps adorned with evangelical symbols so common in the Catacombs" (p. 56).

[2] *Church in Roman Empire*, p. 57. Harnack says : " We are able to-day, on the basis of fully authenticated records, to declare, with satisfactory certainty, that even in the time of the Apostles the palace of the Emperor was one of the chief seats of the growing Christian Church in Rome." Art. on "Christianity and Christians at the Court of the Emperors," in *Princeton Review*, July, 1878, p. 257.

EARLY PROGRESS OF CHRISTIANITY 117

surmised from an obscure notice in Tacitus, which relates how in A.D. 57, a lady of illustrious birth, Pomponia Græcina, wife of Aulus Plautius, the conqueror of Britain, was accused before the Senate, and was tried and acquitted before a domestic tribunal on a charge of "foreign superstition" (*superstitionis externæ*), and how her life was thereafter spent in deep gloom.[1] The peculiarity of the charge in this case led to the conjecture that the "foreign superstition" in question was none other than Christianity. So long as it depended solely on this passage, the inference was felt to be precarious, and we cannot feel surprised that while the majority of scholars acquiesced in it, others, equally learned, took an opposite view. Now, however, the conjecture has practically been converted into certainty by the discovery by De Rossi in the crypt of Lucina—one of

[1] Tac. *Annals*, xiii. 32.

the very oldest parts of the Catacombs—of several inscriptions unmistakably showing a connection of the vault with members of the Pomponian *gens*—one descendant bearing this very family name: Pomponius Græcinus.[1] It is an ingenious conjecture of De Rossi that probably the Lucina who gives her name to the crypt is Pomponia Græcina herself. Lucina would then be the name assumed by this lady at baptism.[2]

This same distinguished person, it should

[1] Cf. Northcote and Brownlow for details, I. pp. 277-281. Lightfoot says, "It is clear therefore that this burial-place was constructed by some Christian lady of rank, probably before the close of the first century, for her fellow-religionists, and that within a generation or two a descendant or near kinsman of Pomponia Græcina was buried." (*Clement*, I. p. 31. Cf. Harnack, *Princeton Review*, July, 1878, p. 263.)

[2] Hasenclever, in his interesting articles on "Christian Proselytes of the Higher Rank in the First Century," in *Jahr. f. Prot. Theol.* viii., seeks to minimise the evidence in the above and later cases, but in view of the Catacomb testimony, his arguments need scarcely be discussed. Cf. Lightfoot, *Clement*, pp. 30, 32, &c.

be said, is connected by many scholars with the gospel in another way, though much weight, I fear, cannot be allowed to their speculations. Specious grounds have been alleged for the identification of the Pudens and Claudia named in 2 Tim. iv. 21 as prominent members of the Church of Rome with a Pudens and Claudia repeatedly mentioned in the epigrams of Martial,[1] the former a Roman centurion of distinction, the latter a British princess whom Pudens wedded. Last century (1722) there was discovered at Chichester an inscription which tells how a site was presented by one Pudens to the British king, Claudius Cogidubnus—the same with whom, as we learn from Tacitus, Aulus Plautius had friendly relations in his campaigns. The presumption is strong that the

[1] See the passages quoted in Alford's Excursus on Pudens and Claudia, in Proleg. to 2 Timothy, *Greek Test.*, iii. p. 104.

Pudens of Martial is an officer who served under Plautius in Britain, and that the princess he married was the daughter of this King Claudius Cogidubnus. If so, we have a link connecting her with Pomponia Græcina, under whose protection it may be presumed that she journeyed to Rome, and whose connection with the family of the Rufi furnishes a reason for the assumption by her of the second name she bears—Claudia *Rufina*. The same link connects Claudia with Christianity, and gives plausibility to the suggestion that through Pomponia she may have been introduced into Christian circles, and with her, Pudens.[1] The weak point in this train of reasoning, otherwise so seductive, is the absence of any evidence that Claudia Rufina *was* brought under Christian influences, for

[1] The Pudens and Claudia of Martial were not married at the date of the epistle; neither apparently were the pair in the text, since the name of Linus intervenes.

the mere occurrence of two names so common as Pudens and Claudia in 2 Tim. iv. 21 does not prove it. The identification with the members of the Roman Church is favoured, however, by writers like Alford, Conybeare and Howson, Lewin, and Plumptre; while Lightfoot and others, on chronological and moral grounds, decidedly—possibly too decidedly—reject it.[1] The utmost that can be said for it at present is that the coincidences are unquestionably striking.

Pomponia Græcina lived on into the reign of Domitian, and her influence, as Lightfoot suggests,[2] may not have been without its share in bringing about the next outstanding cases of conversion we have to record

---

[1] See in favour of the identification, Alford *ut supra* and against, Lightfoot, *Clement*, I. pp. 76-79. Lightfoot gives the references to the others. Farrar, who scouts the identification in his *St. Paul* (ch. 56), uses it to garnish his picture in his *Darkness and Dawn*.

[2] Pp. 32-3.

—those of Flavius Clemens, the consul, and Domitilla, his wife—the former the cousin, the latter the niece, of the Emperor Domitian. The basis here again is the statement of a heathen writer. Dion Cassius (or his epitomiser Xiphilinus) informs us that these two persons were accused of "atheism," and "going astray after the customs of the Jews" (ἀθεότητος . . . ἐς τὰ Ιουδαίων ἔθη ἐξοκέλλοντες), for which offence Clement was put to death, and Domitilla was banished to the island of Pandatereia in the Ægean.[1] The peculiar wording of the charge long ago suggested that, as in the previous case, it was really the offence of Christianity for which Clement and his wife suffered[2]; and

[1] Dion Cassius, lxvii. 44 : Suet. *Dom.* 15. See on these passages Lightfoot, *Philippians*, pp. 21–23 : *Clement*, I. pp. 33–35 : *Ignat.* I. pp. 12, 13.

[2] Thus already Gibbon (ch. xvi.) : "A singular association of ideas, which cannot with any propriety be applied except to the Christians." Most modern scholars agree.

EARLY PROGRESS OF CHRISTIANITY 123

this conjecture was strengthened by a notice in Eusebius, derived from the Roman historian Bruttius, that Flavia Domitilla, whom by a confusion he calls the niece (not the wife) of Flavius Clemens, was banished for confessing Christ.[1] It has been reserved for Catacomb exploration to clear up the ambiguity attaching to this case also, and to establish beyond doubt the Christianity of the illustrious pair. The cemetery of Domitilla has been discovered by the labours of De Rossi, with inscriptions abundantly attesting her ownership of the ground, and its use for Christian burial[2]; while the

[1] Eus. *Ecc. Hist.* iii. 18 : cf. *Chronicle* under A.D. 95. On the discrepancies with Dion Cassius, &c., see Lightfoot, *Phil.*, pp. 22, 23, and *Clement*, I. pp. 44–51 ; and Harnack, *Princeton Review*, July, 1878, pp. 266–69. Harnack favours the theory of two Domitillas.

[2] Cf. for details, Northcote and Brownlow, *Rom. Sott.* I. pp. 120–6 : Lanciani, *Pag. and Christ. Rome*, pp. 316, 335–340 : Lightfoot, *Clement*, I. pp. 35–37 ;

further discovery of an elegantly-constructed crypt of the Flavians shows that, in the words of Harnack, "an entire branch of the Flavian family embraced the Christian faith."[1] It will not be denied that these facts furnish startling illustration of the extent to which, by the close of the first century, Christianity had pushed its conquests. Next to the Emperor himself, these two personages held the highest rank in the Empire; they stood nearest to the throne; their two sons had even been designated by Domitian as his heirs to the purple.[2] It

Harnack, *Princeton Review*, July, 1878, pp. 268–9. The cemetery is that of Domitilla, who alone is mentioned by Eusebius, but the charge was the same against both husband and wife.

[1] Harnack (*ut supra*) says, "What a change! Between fifty and sixty years after Christianity reached Rome, a daughter of the Emperor (Vespasian) embraces the faith, and thirty years after the fearful persecutions of Nero, the presumptive heirs to the throne were brought up in a Christian house" (p. 269).   [2] Suet. *Dom.* 15.

seemed almost as if, ere the last Apostle had quitted the scene of his labours, Christianity were about to mount the seat of empire!

There is, however, yet another case, belonging to this period, quite as striking in its elements of surprise as that of Clemens and Flavia Domitilla. Dion informs us in the passage already cited that besides these two, "many others" ($ἄλλοι\ πολλοί$) were arraigned on the same charges—among them Glabrio who had been consul with Trajan, who also was condemned, and put to death. The full name of this victim of Domitian's persecuting zeal was Manius Acilius Glabrio, and his family was conspicuous as one of the very wealthiest and most illustrious in the State. "Towards the end of the republic," says Lanciani, "we find them (the Acilii) established on the Pincian Hill, where they had built a palace, and laid out gardens which extended at least from the convent of the

Trinità dei Monti to the Villa Borghese. The family had grown so rapidly to honour, splendour, and wealth, that Pertinax in the Senate in which he was elected emperor, proclaimed them the noblest race in the world."[1] Doubt was still entertained by many, however, whether the terms of the passage in Dion necessarily included Christianity among the charges on which Glabrio was condemned, and Lightfoot, in reviewing the evidence, declared that the case seemed to him to break down altogether.[2] It is permissible to think that were this eminent scholar writing now, his opinion would be somewhat modified. For here, again, Catacomb discovery has come to our help. In the year 1888, a crypt was laid bare by the indefatigable De Rossi, which proved to be that of the Acilii Glabriones. A fragment of

[1] *Pagan and Christ. Rome*, p. 5.
[2] *Clement*, I. p. 82.

EARLY PROGRESS OF CHRISTIANITY 127

a marble coffin was found, inscribed with the words *Acilio Glabrioni Filio*,[1] and additional inscriptions have since confirmed the identification.[2] As this crypt forms the centre of a large group of galleries, its Christian character can hardly be doubted. Thus again we see Christianity penetrating into one of the wealthiest and most renowned families of the Flavian age.[3]

The individual instances I have cited are

[1] Probably son of Manius Acilius Glabrio, Consul, 124 A.D. On the Acilian inscriptions, see Frontispiece and Note in Appendix.

[2] Lanciani, pp. 4-8. "His end helped, no doubt," this writer says, "the propagation of the gospel among his relatives and descendants, as well as among the servants and freedmen of the house, as shown by the noble sarcophagi and the humble loculi found in such numbers in the crypt of the Catacombs of Priscilla" (p. 7. Cf. Ramsay, *Church in Roman Empire*, pp. 262-3).

[3] A Catacomb inscription furnishes good reason also for believing that Bruttius, the historian on whom Eusebius depends for his information about Domitilla, was, or became, a Christian. Thus Lightfoot and Lanciani.

far from exhausting the evidence supplied by the Catacombs to the acceptance of the gospel by persons of the upper ranks in society in the first century, but they may suffice. As an interesting indication from the literary side, I may refer to the apocryphal *Acts of Paul and Thecla*, which most scholars now believe to have at least a basis of historical truth. Thecla was the daughter of a noble and wealthy family in Iconium, and Queen Tryphæna, of Pontus, who is shown by recent discovery to be a real historical personage, is related to have been converted by her. Prof. Ramsay accepts these facts as probably historical[1]; Harnack also regards the book as "without doubt resting upon historical accounts."[2] It therefore adds its grain of testimony to our general contention.

[1] *Church in Roman Empire*, p. 414.
[2] *Princeton Review*, July, 1878, p. 263.

When we pass to the second century we are not so entirely dependent upon Catacomb witness as in the first, though here also, as we shall see, the Catacombs have important aid to offer us. The river of Church History still flows, indeed, so much underground as to be for long periods almost entirely out of sight. Yet numerous illustrations are not wanting to show us that the gospel was drawing its converts on every side from the higher as well as the lower orders of society. Pliny, it will be remembered, bears emphatic testimony to this in Bithynia and Pontus. Persons of all ages, *of all ranks*, and of both sexes, he reports to Trajan, had accepted Christianity, and the number was daily increasing.[1] The Epistle of Ignatius to the Romans, about the same time, presupposes, as Dr. Lightfoot points out, that there were persons in high quarters in Rome so in-

[1] Ep., 96.

fluential that the writer fears their intercession may deprive him of the crown of Martyrdom.[1] Hermas, in his *Shepherd*—that *Pilgrim's Progress* of the Early Church—has numerous references to the wealthy in the Church of Rome—possessors of lands and houses—whom he rebukes for worldliness and luxury.[2] The wealth of the Church is witnessed to us in a more pleasing way by its reputation for an abundant liberality. Dionysius, the Bishop of Corinth, about 170 A.D., extols the Church of Rome for this grace. "For this," he says, "is your practice from the beginning, to do good to all the brethren in various ways, and to send

[1] *Ep. to Rom.*, 1, 2 ; cf. Lightfoot, *Ignat.* I. p. 356. To the same effect Harnack : " Before what other person than the Emperor could this intercession be made. . . . We must conclude that there were persons at that time among the Roman Christians who possessed great influence at the Court" (*Princeton Review*, July, 1878, p. 278).

[2] Hermas, *Sim.* i. ; ii. ; viii. 9 ; ix. 20, &c. His own mistress was a rich lady.

contributions to many churches in every city, thus refreshing the poverty of those in need, and furnishing supplies to the brethren in the mines. By these gifts, which ye send from the beginning, as Romans, ye maintain the ancestral custom of the Romans, which your blessed Bishop Soter has not only observed, but also increased, providing great abundance for distribution to the saints, and with blessed words encouraging the brethren from abroad, as a loving father his children."[1] When we reflect that the bulk of the Roman mob was practically idle —clamouring for bread and games, or dangling as clients in attendance on the rich—and that slaves had little, we see that a considerable portion of the membership of the Church must have been composed of persons in higher social station, or at least of the sections which possessed wealth.

[1] Euseb., *Ecc. Hist.*, iv. 23.

Justin's picture of the Christian worship bears out this idea. "The wealthy among us," he says, "help the needy. . . . They who are well to do, and willing, give what each thinks fit; and what is collected is deposited with the president, who succours the orphans and widows, and those who, through sickness or any other cause, are in want, and those who are in bonds, and the strangers sojourning among us."[1]

This brings us again to the corroborative testimony of the Catacombs, and to the interesting additional information which they supply. I can only draw attention to the costly crypts and tombs of the cemetery of Prætextatus—a Catacomb of the second century—which are constructed in the finest style of art.[2] In a tomb cased with marble,

[1] 1st Apol., 67.

[2] See the remarkable descriptions of the architecture, paintings, and rich tombs in Northcote and Brownlow, I. pp. 133-44.

EARLY PROGRESS OF CHRISTIANITY 133

in one of the chambers of this cemetery, lie two bodies, one wrapped in cloth of gold, the other in purple, while on a grave in the wall is an inscription marking the resting-place of "Urania, daughter of Herod."[1] It is hardly possible to avoid connecting this Urania with the daughter of the same name of the famous Herod Atticus,[2] whose villa and mausoleum are in the immediate neighbourhood. If so, the identification is one of the most remarkable we have yet met with. Herod Atticus is known to history as a celebrated rhetorician, and the tutor of Marcus Aurelius, but also,

[1] Northcote and Brownlow, I. p. 134.

[2] "Daughter of Herod Atticus by his second wife, Vibullia Alcia" (Lanciani, *Pagan and Christ. Rome*, p. 9). For a full account of Herod Atticus and his extraordinary wealth, see the same work, pp. 287 ff. Herod's father, through the discovery of a treasure, "suddenly became the richest man in Greece, and probably in the world." Cf. also Merivale, *Romans under the Empire*, ch. lxvi.

through the inheritance of an immense treasure, as probably the wealthiest man of his time. And here we have apparent evidence that his daughter had embraced the Christian faith. We have, besides, inscriptions attesting the Christianity of members of consular families, and many of equestrian rank.[1] A special interest attaches to the discovery by De Rossi, in the cemetery of Callistus, of the crypt of Cæcilia, the virgin-martyr round whom so many legends of the Roman Church subsequently gathered. Some obscurity rests on the date of Cæcilia's martyrdom, but it was probably in the reign of Marcus Aurelius.[2] De Rossi's account of this lady, which Lightfoot in the main accepts, is briefly as follows: That Cæcilia was a lady of noble birth; that the land

[1] *Pagan and Christian Rome*, p. 10.

[2] See the questions fully discussed in Lightfoot, *Ignatius*, I. pp. 503-4.

in this place belonged to her *gens* ; that some members of the family were converted to Christianity in the second century, so that Cæcilia was a Christian from her cradle ; that these Christian Cæcilii made over the subterranean vaults for the purposes of Christian burial, and subsequently were themselves laid here ; and that this was the origin of the cemetery of Callistus, or of parts of it.[1] There is no question in view of the inscriptions found that the crypt discovered by De Rossi is that in which the body of the martyr was originally laid, and from which it is related to have been removed with honour by Pope Paschal in the ninth century.[2] The spread of Christianity in the

[1] Lightfoot, *ut supra*.

[2] The body was placed in the Church of St. Cæcilia in Trastevere. In 1599, in the course of excavations, the marble sarcophagus, with the body enclosed, clothed in blood-stained robes of golden tissue, was brought to light. Cf. Northcote and Brownlow, I. pp. 320-1.

gens is abundantly attested by the numbers of epitaphs of these Christian Cæcilii and other noble families connected with them by blood and marriage in adjoining parts of the Catacomb, and these not mere dependents, but, as their titles, *Clarissimus*, *Clarissima*, and the like, show, illustrious members of their houses.[1]

All this speaks with great distinctness to the highly influential position of the Church at Rome, and if we cannot pronounce with the same definiteness of other places, it is only because, till near the end of the century, light almost wholly fails us. When we do get a glimpse, as in the beautiful Epistle of the Churches of Vienne and Lyons, giving an account of the martyr-

[1] Northcote and Brownlow, I. pp. 278, 327. Twelve or thirteen of these epitaphs, all of Cæcilii or Cæciliani, are found in the crypt of Lucina. There seems further to have been some connection between this family and that of Pomponia Græcina.

doms in these places in 177 A.D., the same mixture of classes is forced on our attention. If we have Blandina, the slave-girl, a "noble athlete" in confessing Christ, we have also among the sufferers the mistress of Blandina; we have one prominent confessor, noted as "a man of distinction" ($\dot{\epsilon}\pi\dot{\iota}\sigma\eta\mu o\varsigma$); we have a number of Roman citizens; we have heads of households, whose domestics are seized to give evidence against them; we have a well-known physician; and generally the martyrs seem to be of the middle or better class.[1] Another remarkable instance—again from Rome—is that of the senator Apollonius, a man "renowned for learning and philosophy," who, on being denounced by an informer, made an eloquent defence of his religion before the Senate, and was sentenced to decapitation.[2] When, however, we

[1] See the Epistle in Eusebius, v. 1.
[2] Eus. v. 21. The Acts of Apollonius have re-

approach the close of the century, full light returns to us; and we see in the Churches of Carthage and Alexandria, and elsewhere, how completely Christianity had succeeded in penetrating the wealthiest classes in the chief centres of population.

The fatal edict (or, as Neumann will have it, rescript[1]) of Septimus Severus, in 202 A.D., which initiated the persecution connected with his name, came as a great revealing blow to the Churches affected by it. It made manifest, not only how many of the wealthier and dignified classes had, nominally at least, embraced Christianity, but also how unfit much of their profession was to endure the fire of trial. Here it may be noted as singular that the brunt of the persecution

cently been recovered. Cf. Conybeare, *The Armenian Apology and Acts of Apollonius* (1896); then, after the discovery of the *Greek* Acts, Klette, *Der Process und Die Acta S. Apollonius* (1897).

[1] *Der Röm. Staat*, p. 161.

EARLY PROGRESS OF CHRISTIANITY 139

was borne, not by the Church of Rome, but by the comparatively remote Churches of North Africa and Egypt. The same thing may be observed in other persecutions. Why was this? Was it that the Roman Christian community was socially obscure and insignificant? Or was it for the opposite reason, which Tertullian suggests, that Christianity had struck its roots so deeply into the State, and had drawn to itself in Rome so many illustrious men and women—people in the highest positions [1]—that even an emperor might shrink from the upturning of society which a general proscription would involve? Septimus Severus himself, as we know, for a time looked favourably on Christianity, having been healed, it is said, of some disorder by a Christian slave.[2] Whatever the explanation, the blow did fall pre-eminently, not on the capital, but on Carthage and

[1] *Ad Scapulam*, 4. [2] Ibid.

Alexandria, and its effect in both places was to discover at once the hold which the new religion had on the people of rank and wealth. Tertullian is an unexceptionable witness for Carthage. In his address to the proconsul Scapula, pleading his cause with that dignitary, he pictures the Christians presenting themselves in a body before his tribunal, and asks, " What will you make of so many thousands, of such a multitude of men and women, persons of every sex, and every age, and every rank, when they present themselves before you? How many fires, how many swords will be required? What will be the anguish of Carthage itself, which you will have to decimate, as each one recognises there his relatives and companions, as he sees there, it may be, men of your own order, and noble ladies, and all the leading persons of the city, and either kinsmen or friends of those of your own circle? Spare thyself, if not us poor

EARLY PROGRESS OF CHRISTIANITY 141

Christians! Spare Carthage, if not thyself!"[1] When the storm burst, it was naturally those classes which had to make the greatest worldly sacrifices which showed the largest number of defections. If they did not deny Christ, they sought by expedients of bribery to secure exemption from trouble. "Whole churches," says Tertullian, in this way "imposed tribute *en masse* on themselves."[2]

Clearest of all among the proofs, however, of the extent to which the wealth and fashion of these luxurious cities had found their way into the Churches, are the satirical descriptions and denunciations of Tertullian and Clement of Alexandria in picturing a state of Christian society deeply infected with the vices and follies of the age. The rules of living in Clement's *Pædagogue*, with their "caustic sketches," to use Farrar's words, "of the glutton, and

[1] *Ad Scap.* 5.   [2] *De Fuga*, 13.

the dandy, and the painted, perfumed, bewigged, and bejewelled lady of fashion,"[1] would have no application at all to a Church composed wholly or mainly of "dregs of the populace"; and the same may be said of Tertullian's denunciation of the luxury and extravagance of the women of his time in his tract on *The Attire of Women*.[2] Dean Milman takes what seems the only just view of the matter. "It appears unquestionable," he says, "that the strength of Christianity lay in the middle, perhaps the mercantile, classes. The last two books of the *Pædagogue* of Clement of Alexandria, the most copious authority for Christian manners at that time,

[1] *The Fathers*, I. p. 375.
[2] Cf., *e.g.*, the picture of extravagance in the close of bk. i., and the denunciations of cosmetics, dyeing the hair, elaborate hair-attire, splendid and excessive dress, in bk. ii., with the concession to those "whom the exigencies of riches, or birth, or past dignities, compel to appear in public so gorgeously arrayed as not to appear to have attained wisdom " (ii. 9).

EARLY PROGRESS OF CHRISTIANITY 143

inveigh against the vices of an opulent and luxurious community; splendid dresses, jewels, gold and silver vessels, rich banquets, gilded litters and chariots, and private baths. The ladies kept Indian birds, Median peacocks, monkeys, and Maltese dogs, instead of maintaining widows and orphans, the men had multitudes of slaves. The sixth chapter of the third book (that the Christian alone is rich) would have been unmeaning if addressed to a poor community."[1]

But if many were vain and foolish, and fell in the stress of the persecutions, there were honourable exceptions. The gem of the martyrology of this period is the undoubtedly genuine narrative[2] of the martyrdom of Perpetua and her companions. Perpetua, a young married lady, of noble birth, was, with her brother, a catechumen

[1] *Hist. of Christ.*, ii., ch. ix. (note).
[2] Cf. *Acts*, written partly by Perpetua herself.

of the Church at Carthage.[1] Thrown into prison, and tried in the sorest way a woman can be, through the entreaties of her aged father, and the tenderest appeals to her motherhood, she yet, through all, remained constant. With her perished four others, one of them, Felicitas, a slave. Here, again, high-born and humble receive together the baptism of blood. In the life of Origen, to name other instances, we remember gratefully that "certain lady, of great wealth and distinction," in Alexandria, who showed him kindness after his father's martyrdom[2]; that other wealthy lady Juliana, in whose house he was sheltered in Cappadocia[3]; and his friend, Ambrose, himself afterwards a martyr for Christ, who, out of his abundance, furnished him with books, scribes, shorthand

[1] Or Tuburbium.   [2] Eus. vi. 2.
[3] Ibid., vi. 17. Palladius supplements this notice on the authority of an entry in a book by Origen himself.

EARLY PROGRESS OF CHRISTIANITY 145

writers, and every facility for pursuing his Biblical studies.[1]

The name of Origen recalls attention to another series of facts intimately bearing on our present subject. I refer to the relations subsisting between Christianity and the Imperial Court. These, probably, had never quite ceased from the days of the Flavians, but we find them renewed towards the close of the second century, and perpetuating themselves during nearly the whole of the third. A commencement is made in the reign of Commodus, the unworthy son of Marcus Aurelius. Marcia, the favourite mistress of this emperor, was the foster-daughter of a Christian presbyter, and, even in her equivocal position, seems to have retained her interest in Christianity. On one occasion we know of, she was instrumental in procuring by her intercession the release

[1] Eus. vi. 18, 23.

146 NEGLECTED FACTORS IN THE

of certain Christian confessors from the Sardinian mines.[1] There would seem, in fact, to have been in this reign a general movement in the upper classes towards the new faith. Eusebius records that " many of those highly distinguished in wealth and family, with their whole house and kindred, turned to their salvation "[2]; and Irenæus speaks freely of the faithful in the Imperial palace.[3] Septimus Severus, the next important emperor, was, as we saw, at first not unfavourably affected to the Christian religion. His Syrian wife, Julia Domna, cultured and syncretistic in spirit, seems also to have been friendly.[4] Their son, Caracalla, had a

[1] Hippolytus, *Phil.* ix. 12.

[2] Eus. v. 21. To this reign belongs the martyrdom of the senator Apollonius referred to above.

[3] *Adv. Hær.* iv. 30.

[4] Cf. Uhlhorn's *Conflict of Christ.*, p. 333 (E.T.); Baur's *History of Church*, II. p. 207 (E.T.) ; Bigg's *Christian Platonists of Alexandria*, p. 244. See next lecture.

EARLY PROGRESS OF CHRISTIANITY 147

Christian nurse—was fed, as was said, on Christian milk.[1] Julia's influence may be regarded as propagating itself in the reigns of the succeeding emperors. We find Hippolytus addressing a treatise to Julia Aquila, the second wife of the infamous Elagabulus.[2] Julia Mammæa, niece of Julia Domna, mother of the next emperor, Alexander Severus, who exercised a large control in the government, was deeply interested in Christianity, and sent for Origen to Antioch to confer with her.[3] Alexander himself honoured Christ by placing His statue in his private chapel along with those of other sages, and had His Golden Rule inscribed on the walls of his palace and public monuments.[4] A succeeding emperor, Philip the

[1] Tert., *Ad Scap.* 4.
[2] See Moeller, *Church History*, I. pp. 191, 201, (E.T.).   [3] Eus. vi. 21.
[4] Lampridius, *Sev. Alex.* Cf. in Gieseler (I. p. 192, E.T.) and Neander, I. p. 173 (Bohn).

Arabian, was so favourable to Christianity that he was publicly reputed to be a Christian.[1] Origen is related to have had correspondence with him and with his wife Severa.[2] Dionysius of Alexandria could write of the early years of Valerian, even after the Church had passed through the fiery trial of the Decian persecution, that none of the emperors before him had been so favourably and kindly disposed to the Christians, "not even those who were openly said to be Christians" (Philip); and that "his house was filled with pious persons, and was, indeed, a Church (ἐκκλησία) of the Lord."[3] A new spirit, in fact, began to manifest itself in this period towards Christianity, in con-

[1] Eus. vi. 34. Cf. in Gieseler, I. p. 192. Some modern writers, as Aubé, Moeller, favour this view. Cf. Moeller, *Church History*, I. p. 192 (E.T.).

[2] Eus. vi. 36.

[3] Ibid. vii. 10. Valerian subsequently became a persecutor.

EARLY PROGRESS OF CHRISTIANITY 149

trast with the spirit of contempt which had formerly prevailed, the spirit of eclecticism and toleration—the intellectual counterpart of which is seen in Neo-Platonism.[1] Under these circumstances, Origen could boast that some addition was made to the numbers of the Christians every day, and that in the multitude of believers were numbered "not only rich men, but persons of rank and delicate and high-born ladies."[2] Eusebius also speaks of "the wealthy and opulent" in the Church of Rome at the time of the Novatian schism[3] in the middle of the century.

It was clearly enough perceived, however, by thoughtful men like Origen, that the final victory would not come without a terrible closing struggle. This time of testing soon arrived. The Decian persecution broke over the Church, discovering, as before, the

[1] See Lect. III.   [2] *Contra Celsum,* vii. 26; III. 9.
[3] Eus. vi. 43.

numbers of persons of wealth and rank within its pale, but proving also the frailty of their profession. The well-known passage of Dionysius of Alexandria gives us a vivid picture of the behaviour of these apostates. When brought to the altar, after the edict had actually been promulgated, "all were greatly alarmed," he says, "and many of the more eminent came immediately forward in their fear; others, holding public offices, were drawn on by their duties; others were urged on by those about them. When called by name, they approached the impure and unholy sacrifices, some pale and trembling, not as sacrificers, but as if they were themselves to be sacrifices and victims to the idols, so that they were jeered at by the large multitude that stood around, as it was plain to all that they were afraid either to die or to sacrifice; but some advanced more readily to the altars, stoutly asserting that they had never before been Christians."[1] More eloquent than any statement of Church historians, however, is the language of the persecuting edicts themselves. That of Valerian, after he had assumed the *rôle* of a persecutor (A.D. 258), is specially directed against office-bearers and persons of high rank in the Church.[2] It ordains "that bishops, presbyters, and deacons be immediately put to death; that senators and men of rank and knights be first of all deprived of their rank and property, and then, their means being taken away, if they still continue to be Christians, be also punished with death; that matrons, after forfeiting their property be banished; that those in Cæsar's household who have formerly made profession of Christianity, or now profess it, be treated as Cæsar's property, and, being put in chains,

[1] Eus. vi. 41.
[2] It is given in Cyprian's Epistle to Successus (Ep. 80).

be distributed among the Imperial estates." We are, accordingly, not surprised to learn from Dionysius that amongst the victims of this persecution were "men and women, young and old, young virgins and aged matrons, soldiers and private persons of every kind and every age." He himself was an example of one who had repeatedly had experience of "confiscations, proscriptions, plunderings of goods, loss of dignities."[1]

The forty years' peace which elapsed between this persecution and the last decisive struggle in the Diocletian persecution furnishes us with few details, yet with suggestive general notices of the continued growth of the churches in numbers, splendour, and influence, one marked outward token of this prosperity being the number of splendid

[1] Eus. vii. 11. As respects the order of knights, Lanciani mentions that hundreds of inscriptions of persons of equestrian rank are found in the Catacombs (p. 10).

ecclesiastical edifices which now began to be erected. We read of Christian governors of provinces, and of the freedom to profess Christianity granted to the members of the Imperial household—"wives, and children, and servants."[1] Mention is made of the multitudes crowding in every city to the houses of worship—"on whose account," says the historian, "not being content with the ancient buildings, they erected spacious churches from the foundation in all the cities."[2] That this is not an exaggeration is shown by the great church in Nicomedia, which appears to have been one of the architectural ornaments of this city—the seat of the Court at the time—and by the later edicts for the demolition of the churches generally.[3] Yet instances exist to show that Christians were not entirely safe even during

[1] Eus. viii. 1. Instances are given. [2] Ibid. Lactantius, *De Morte Per.* 12 ; Eus., *Ecc. Hist.* viii. 2.

this interval of peace. We know at least of one illustrious Roman officer at Cæsarea who suffered death for his faith; and we read also of how one Astyrius, a Roman of senatorial rank, in high favour with the Emperor, and well known to all for his noble birth and wealth, took the body of the martyred man, and, covering it with a splendid and costly dress, gave it becoming burial.[1]

The great accession of members and outwardly prosperous condition of the Church at this time is beyond dispute, and the incidents of the last and most dreadful of the persecutions only furnish new corroborations of it. During the first nineteen years of his reign, Diocletian had Christians everywhere about his person. Some of the officers of highest rank in his palace were Christians[2];

[1] Eus. vii. 15, 16.
[2] Ibid. viii. 6. Such was Lucianus, the chief cham-

his own wife and daughter, Prisca and Valeria, were believed to be Christians.[1] The first persecuting edict was directed against the church buildings and the Scriptures rather than against persons; but it ordains also that those holding honourable positions were to be degraded, and servants in the household, if they persisted in their Christianity, were to be made slaves.[2] What one notices with satisfaction in this persecution is the superior steadfastness of believers in the higher orders, as contrasted with the frailty of this class on previous occasions. Many of the most illustrious martyrs of Diocletian's reign are persons of exalted rank. Such were some of the great officers of the palace, of whose sufferings and constancy a special account

berlain, to whom Theonas, Bishop of Alexandria, wrote a letter of advice. See the account in Neander, I. pp. 197-9 (Bohn).

[1] Lact. 15.   [2] Eus. viii. 2.

is given.[1] Such were the martyrs of the Thebais, many of them, as Eusebius tells, "distinguished for wealth, and noble birth and honour, and excelling in philosophy and learning"[2]; such was Adanetus, of Phrygia, a man of noble Italian family, "who had been advanced through every honour by the emperors," and had reputably filled the highest offices[3]; such were certain ladies of Antioch, "illustrious above all for wealth, for family, for reputation"[4]—and many more of whom these are but examples. A striking instance, referred to in the previous lecture, is that of a town in Phrygia which was burned with all its inhabitants because its whole population, including the governors and magistrates, with all the men of rank, had confessed themselves Christians, and refused to sacrifice.[5] It may be remem-

[1] Eus. viii. 6.   [2] Ibid. viii. 9.   [3] Ibid. viii. 11.
[4] Ibid. viii. 12.   [5] Ibid. viii. 11.

bered also how the Council of Elvira, in Spain, in 306, shows us great landowners and persons in the highest magistracies in the membership of the Church.

There is only one other line of evidence to which, in closing, I would advert for a moment, as bearing on this question of the penetration by the gospel of the higher ranks of society. It is that furnished by the social station of the great teachers of the Church. That these, like the earlier Apologists, were men of education and refinement is a fact which of itself implies a standing sufficiently high to secure for them the advantages of a liberal training. But we have only to recall the facts of their lives to be reminded that many of them in reality sprang from families of wealth and distinction. Tertullian was the son of a proconsular centurion—no very high rank perhaps—but enough to obtain for him the benefits of a legal and rhetorical education.

We are probably right in saying that Clement of Alexandria was the son of wealthy parents. His culture and extensive travels would seem to imply as much. Cyprian, we know, was of patrician descent, and inherited large possessions. Two other distinguished teachers of the third century—both pupils of Origen— Dionysius of Alexandria and Gregory Thaumaturgus, were of wealthy and honourable families. So was Pamphilus of Cæsarea, the friend of Eusebius, and founder of the famous library in that city. It is going beyond our present limits to extend our view to the fourth century, but if we do so we have such conspicuous instances as Basil the Great of Cæsarea and his brother Gregory of Nyssa, as Ambrose of Milan, as Chrysostom of Antioch, and many others that might be named. I trust, however, I have already said enough to show the baselessness of the theory that the bulk of the adherents of early Christianity were drawn from " the dregs of the populace," and to demonstrate that the gospel from its earliest beginnings in no slight degree affected the higher as well as the humbler classes of society.

THE *INTENSIVE* OR *PENETRATIVE*
INFLUENCE OF CHRISTIANITY ON
THE THOUGHT AND LIFE OF THE
EMPIRE.

The instreaming of Pagan influences on Christianity has for its counterpart the outstreaming of Christian influences on Pagan society—These also ordinarily under-estimated — Silence of Pagan writers : what it means—Christianity and culture in the First Century—New Testament Epistles—Seneca and the Gospel—Rise and character of Apology in the Second Century— The literary attack on Christianity : Celsus— Significance and spread of Gnosticism—The Pagan ethical revival in Second Century — Pagan preaching—Influence of Christianity on these—The Mysteries—The old Catholic Fathers —Rise of Neo-Platonism—Effects of Christianity on morals and legislation—Conclusion.

LECTURE III

THE *INTENSIVE* OR *PENETRATIVE* INFLUENCE OF CHRISTIANITY ON THE THOUGHT AND LIFE OF THE EMPIRE

PROFESSOR HARNACK has said: "The Catholic Church is that form of Christianity in which every element of the ancient world has been successively assimilated which Christianity could in any way take up into itself without utterly losing itself in the world. . . . Christianity has throughout sucked the marrow of the ancient world, and assimilated it."[1] If

[1] Art. on "Research in Early Church History" in *Cont. Rev.*, Aug. 1886, p. 234.

this dictum of Harnack's is correct, the counter thesis must hold good, that Christianity must have penetrated deeply into the thought and life of the ancient world before such assimilation was possible. Before, for instance, Christianity could suck the marrow out of Greek philosophy, as Harnack supposes it did, it must have penetrated into minds possessed with the spirit and ideas of that philosophy—must have entered deeply into the circles and schools of culture. I am to ask in the present lecture how far this penetrative process went, and what traces it has left of itself in history.

Our previous inquiries have an important bearing on the subject now to be investigated. If it were the case that Christianity had only an insignificant fraction of the population in its following,—if its adherents were collected chiefly from the base and servile classes,—if it was practically unheeded and well-nigh totally despised by persons of higher station and better culture for at least the first two centuries, it would be natural to conclude that traces of its influence on society would be scarcely perceptible, and that what look like such traces must be explained in some other way. We must hold with Friedländer that "it is scarcely thinkable that in the heathen world before the time of Severus, the world-historical importance of the new religion, so little regarded and so contemptuously judged of, was even so much as suspected."[1] But if, as I have endeavoured to show, the case was far different,—if Christianity had both a larger following, and was drawing its adherents from the higher and educated classes to a much greater extent than is commonly assumed,—then we are prepared to entertain the

[1] *Sittengeschichte Roms,* III. p. 536.

expectation that the traces of its action on the Pagan world will be neither few nor slight.

There is a point of considerable moment in this connection to which it is desirable that attention should be directed at the outset. Much stress is often laid (*e.g.* by Friedländer[1]), in disproof of any considerable influence of Christianity on the thought and life of the time, on the silence of Pagan writers respecting the new religion. How, it is asked, if Christianity was so powerful a factor as we hold it to have been in the second century, should a philosophic writer like Marcus Aurelius, for example, pass it by with only one contemptuous reference? This silence

[1] See his argument, Ibid., p. 533. "Christians and Christianity," he says, "till near the end of the second century, are, in the classic literature, only very seldom and incidentally, indifferently and contemptuously mentioned." Similarly Addis, in *Christianity and the Roman Empire*, p. 51, "Epictetus and M. Aurelius dismiss it with a scornful phrase," &c.

of heathen writers is not quite so great as is assumed—Pliny was not silent, nor Fronto, nor Celsus—but even if the fact were as stated, there is one important consideration which greatly takes away the point from the argument. Nothing is better ascertained than that it was the fashion of heathen writers, even of those who were best acquainted with Christianity, to show their contempt for it, by deliberately dissembling their knowledge of it, and refraining from any mention of it in their works. Prof. Ramsay has noticed this in regard to Dion Cassius, who wrote in the third century, when it will not be denied that Christianity was a growing and formidable force, but who seems studiously to have refrained from referring to the Christians in his history; and to Ælius Aristides, the famous rhetorician, a contemporary of Polycarp under the Antonines, who likewise makes a point of not mentioning the Christians (testified to be so numerous and influential in Asia Minor by Pliny), but speaks of them generally as "those in Palestine." "It was apparently a fashion and an affectation," Prof. Ramsay says, "among a certain class of Greek men of letters about 160-240 to ignore the existence of the Christians, and to pretend to confuse them with the Jews."[1] It was not, however, I would observe, a fashion confined to this period, and to Greek writers; and did not apply only to the Christians, though in their case it was specially noticeable. Boissier warns us against being deceived by the grand airs of disdain and ignorance which the Romans affected for everything which was removed from their habits and traditions.[2] "The conspiracy of

[1] *The Church in the Roman Empire*, p. 264. Friedländer also has no doubt that the passage in Aristides refers to the Christians (III. p. 533).

[2] *La Religion Romaine*, II. p. 59, 4th edit. (bk. ii. ch. 5).

silence," as this writer names it, was maintained, astonishing to say, quite as effectively in the fourth and fifth centuries—long after Christianity had decisively triumphed in the State—as in the second. " Paganism," says Dean Merivale, "abstained studiously from any allusion to the place which Christianity now actually held in public life. It made an effort, a laborious effort, to pass over the phenomenon in complete silence. Throughout the few remains of popular literature of the age of Constantine we can trace, it seems, no single reference to the existence of the Christian Church or Creed. Even at the end of the century, the poet Claudian, in versifying, as is his wont, all the chief events of contemporary history, has not one word to say of the new religion, which in his day had effected a complete revolution both in Church and State." [1] And Claudian here was no

[1] *Epochs of Early Church Hist.*, p. 6.

exception. Speaking of Macrobius, by whom "the name of Christianity is not even once pronounced," Boissier remarks, "Our surprise is redoubled when we find the same silence preserved by nearly all the Pagan writers of this time (fourth and fifth centuries), by grammarians, orators, poets, and even historians, though it appears singular that they should omit, in a narrative of the past, such an event as the triumph of the Church. Neither Aurelius Victor nor Eutropius mentions the conversion of Constantine, and it would seem, to read them, that all the princes of the fourth century persevered in the practice of the ancient worship. It is certainly not chance which leads them all to avoid mentioning the name of a religion which they hate; it is a plot, a party move, the meaning of which can deceive nobody."[1] These un-

[1] *La Fin du Paganisme*, II. p. 243. Cf. also Lightfoot, *Philippians*, pp. 28-29.

questionable facts do away, I think, in great part with the relevancy of any argument derived from the mere silence or contempt of Pagan writers. If M. Aurelius did not mention the Christians, it is not, as we shall immediately see, because he did not know enough about them, but because he did not desire to mention them, or willed to ignore them.

That even in the Apostolic Age Christianity had entered as a ferment into minds possessed of some degree of literary and philosophical culture is evident from the phenomena met with in several of the Apostolic Churches, as well as from the cast and character of the New Testament writings themselves. In Corinth, and Ephesus, and Colosse, *e.g.*, the earlier danger to which the Churches had been exposed, and to which the Churches in Galatia succumbed, of being drawn back into the web of legal bondage, had evidently given place to a new and subtler peril—that of the gospel being brought into dependence on a philosophy foreign to its nature, and spoiled by being mixed up with human speculations, and set forth in the trickery of an artificial rhetoric. It is easy, if we recall the scenes of agitation and disputation amidst which the gospel was introduced into some of these Churches—the conflicts, for instance, around the judgment seat of Gallio,[1] or the two years daily disputation in the school of one Tyrannus at Ephesus,[2] with its sequel in the burning of the magic books —to realise how this should be so. In Corinth it was the alliance with Greek wisdom and heathen rhetoric that was sought; in Colosse it was amalgamation with Essenian and incipient Gnostic ele-

[1] Acts xviii. 12–17. [2] Ibid. xix. 9, 10, 19.

ments that was attempted [1]; but in either case the result was the same—a departure from the purity and simplicity of the gospel —an exaltation of knowledge over piety— and a straying into various paths of intellectual heresy. It is interesting to observe also how the Apostle deals with these aberrations—not by denying the value of knowledge, or the legitimacy of the claim of the mind for satisfaction in the sphere of intelligence, but by affirming the power of Christianity to develop a σοφία of its own, and by setting in their right relations knowledge and love.[2] It is not wisdom as such, but "the wisdom of the world" against which the Apostle's polemic is directed. But the New Testament writings themselves, in their very form and structure, in many instances bear witness to

[1] Cf. Lightfoot's *Colossians*.
[2] 1 Cor. ii. 6, 7 ; viii. 1.

the intellectual atmosphere in which they were produced. The Pauline Epistles, with their deep thought, their closely-knit reasoning, and their views of truth reaching out into the eternities before and after, were, on the face of them, not intended for illiterates or weaklings; the Epistles to the Ephesians and Colossians, with their developments of the cosmological aspects of redemption and their implied references to Gnostic speculations, discover that they are written in view of active heretical tendencies; an unmistakable Alexandrian stamp rests on the Epistle to the Hebrews; and the Fourth Gospel, however profoundly separated in substance from Philonism, yet shows, I cannot but think, in the shape in which its prologue is cast, a desire to create a bridge between the current Logos speculations and the truth as it is in Jesus.

Accepting these facts as indications of

the subtle yet energetic manner in which Christianity was engaging the interest, and penetrating the thought, of intelligent circles in the greater heathen communities, I go on to inquire whether evidences of this can be discovered outside the New Testament in the general Pagan world of the first century. There is no *a priori* reason why they should not be, for, as Boissier remarks, "If De Rossi is right, it is necessary to assume that Christianity was less unknown to the rich and lettered in the first century than is supposed."[1] This inquiry has commonly been associated with the name of Seneca, in the reign of Nero—and not unnaturally, for in Seneca's writings we have at once the best specimens of the ethical thought of that time, and the most singular approximations in sentiment and expression to the new ideas introduced by Christianity. Whether,

[1] *La Rel. Romaine,* II. p. 62 (4th edit.).

or how far, these resemblances are due to any measure of acquaintance with the new religion—to any direct or indirect influence of the gospel spirit — or, again, are an independent development from Stoicism, is a question on which opinions are, and probably will always be, widely divided, and which will tend to be determined according to the presuppositions with which the inquirer sets out.[1] We would not depreciate the splendid services which Stoicism, with its stern and elevated, yet haughty and impassive, doctrine of virtue, its notion of a unity of mankind based on reason, and its cosmopolitan ideals, rendered as a preparation for Christianity ; and we must not overlook the fact that, notwithstanding

[1] Among others the question is discussed by Fleury, Troplong, Aubertin, Lightfoot, Hasenclever, Schmidt, Friedländer, Boissier, and Farrar. The fullest discussion in recent writers is by Boissier and Lightfoot.

apparent coincidences with Christian ideas and phrases, Seneca's thinking is still, at bottom, unchangeably and even crudely Stoical.[1] At first, too, it must be granted, the presumption is strongly against any contact of Seneca with Christianity. The fictitious correspondence of the philosopher with St. Paul is long since given up; there is no evidence that Seneca ever saw or heard of the Apostle, though the possibility of such knowledge cannot be denied[2]; the fact that it was his brother Gallio before whom Paul appeared in Corinth affords but a slender ground for supposing that the details of this incident may have reached Seneca; while the circumstance[3] that Seneca, when Paul reached

[1] See the convincing evidence of this, *e.g.*, in Lightfoot's dissertation on St. Paul and Seneca in his *Philippians*.

[2] The possibility is allowed by Friedländer, &c.

[3] Urged by Hasenclever.

Rome, was already a man of sixty years of age, whose philosophical "Weltanschauung" may be presumed to have been completed, and whose death fell some four years later (A.D. 65), is certainly of considerable weight. It is not contended, however, except by a few, that Seneca's philosophical view ever *was* fundamentally changed. But against these negative considerations there are others of a more positive character which may fairly be placed. Paul was not the only channel through which Seneca may have derived some knowledge of the ethics of the gospel. The Christians, as we saw in the first lecture, were by no means in his day an obscure party in Rome[1]; numbers of them were found in the palace, and among the domestics of the great households, including probably Seneca's own; the sage was in the habit

[1] Cf. Lightfoot, pp. 25, 33.

EARLY PROGRESS OF CHRISTIANITY 179

of familiar converse with his slaves[1]; the recent case of Pomponia Græcina must have been the subject of much conversation in the highest circles[2]; the bonds, and no doubt the preaching of the Apostle were bruited throughout the Prætorium and widely elsewhere, and, in Lightfoot's words, "a marvellous activity" was awakened "among the disciples of the new faith."[3] The Apostle Paul underwent a public trial, at which Seneca may have been present[4]; it is not impossible that even the incident of Gallio may have come to the philosopher's ears, if not otherwise, yet through the mention of it in the tales told of this remarkable

[1] Ep. 47. Cf. Lightfoot, p. 300.

[2] See last lecture.

[3] Lightfoot, p. 32. Not only "throughout the Prætorium," but "to all the rest." "In every way Christ is preached" (Phil. i. 13, 18).

[4] Thus De Rossi. Friedländer questions his argument, III. p. 535.

prisoner. Dr. Lightfoot also mentions,[1] what his quotations bear out, that it is in the later writings of Seneca that these approximations to Christian ideas are most apparent.[2]

All this, however, does not amount to positive proof, and it is on the internal evidence of Seneca's writings that the determination of the probabilities of this question must mainly rest. And here, though on

[1] Pp. 291, 298.

[2] There is a passage in Seneca's Epistles in which he describes some striking influence which had produced a marked change in him. "I perceive, Lucilius," he says, "that I am not only amended, but transformed. . . . I would desire to share with you my change so suddenly experienced." ("Intelligo, Lucili, non amendari me tantum, sed transfigurari . . . cuperem tecum communicare tam subitam mei mutationem," i. 6.) He sends his friend the books which had wrought this change in him, with the passages marked. There is nothing, certainly, to connect these books with Christian writings, but the words are remarkable. The Epistles to Lucilius belong to the last years of his life.

academic grounds it will always be possible
to say about as much against as for any
Christian influence on Seneca, I think the
reasons for presuming some degree of such
influence are exceedingly strong. It remains
the fact, account for it as we may, that about
the middle of this century a warmer and
more tender breath begins to enter into
Stoicism, which, thereafter, continuously
animates it ; a purer conception of God's
Fatherly goodness and beneficent Providence ; a kindlier and gentler tone towards
slaves and dependents ; something like a
religious trust and resignation ; a more
merciful and gracious spirit generally. This
is first perceptible, as far as I know, in the
writings of Seneca, and it is specially perceptible in his later years.[1] We know of one

[1] Troplong remarks, after De Maistre, that Seneca
has written a fine book on Providence, for which
there was not even a name at Rome in the time of
Cicero, and he speaks of the new Stoicism as

cause which would produce this change, while it does not seem to follow naturally from the Stoicism of the remaining parts of Seneca's system, with which it stands rather in striking inconsistency. We are driven back, therefore, on an analysis of the supposed resemblances, and here, after making every reasonable deduction, it is difficult not to agree with Dr. Lightfoot, as the result of his singularly impartial survey, that "a class of coincidences still remains . . . which can hardly be considered accidental,"[1] and of which some measure of acquaintance with Christianity—at least contact with its spirit and teaching in some oral form—affords the

"enveloped, as it were, in the atmosphere of Christianity."—*L'Influence du Christ.*, I. ch. 4. Cf. Merivale's *Romans under the Empire*, ch. liv.

[1] P. 298. Prof. Ramsay, in his *Church in the Roman Empire*, said, "that Seneca had some slight acquaintance with Christian teaching appears to be plain from his writings" (p. 273). His statement in *St. Paul the Traveller* is less positive (ch. xv.).

most natural explanation. I do not attach much importance to the fact, but it is worth mentioning, that a tomb was discovered at Ostia bearing the inscription, " Annæus Paulus Petrus," showing that at a later period (third century) persons belonging to the family of Seneca, possibly descendants of freedmen, were Christians.[1] At a later period, the evidence of the influence of Christianity on this transformed Stoicism is clearer. Epictetus, the lame slave, and noblest representative of second-century Stoicism, refers, indeed, but once to the Christians under the contemptuous name of " Galileans," yet his discourses breathe a remarkable spirit of elevated piety, and Dr. Lightfoot finds in them parallels with the Gospels and writings

[1] The exact words are, "ANNÆO. PAULO. PETRO. ANNÆUS. PAULUS."—De Rossi in *Bull. di Archeol. crist.*, 1867. Cf. Harnack in *Princeton Review*, July, 1878, p. 261 ; Friedländer, III. p. 535. Boissier, Lightfoot, Renan, &c., refer to the inscription.

of Paul, which he can hardly believe to be accidental. On one such coincidence he remarks that, "combined with the numerous parallels in Seneca's writings collected above, it favours the supposition that our Lord's discourses, in some form or another, were early known to heathen writers."[1]

In this second century, to which we now come, we reach a period in which the influence of Christianity on general contemporary thought is no longer a matter of precarious inference, but is attested by a wide range of interesting facts. The principal of these within the Church are the rise of a vigorous and learned Christian Apology, and the development in every form and variety of the heterogeneous systems which we group under the name of Gnosticism; while, in the Empire itself, phenomena present themselves, which, as I believe, are inex-

[1] P. 316.

plicable save through the powerful and still under-estimated penetration by Christianity of the Pagan world of religion and culture.

The second century is peculiarly the age of the Christian Apology. It was an age intensely literary, and, as we shall see, was marked by a powerful religious and ethical revival. The rhetorician, the philosopher, the preacher, the teacher, the declaimer, were everywhere. Under the arrangements instituted by Vespasian for the support of lecturers throughout the provinces and cities, literature took on a new refinement, schools and universities flourished, and thought and speech ran naturally into the forms of rhetorical and philosophical discourse and argument.[1] In harmony with this spirit,

[1] See the sketches of this age in Merivale's *Romans under the Empire*, chs. lx., lxvi.; and in Renan's *Marc-Aurèle*, ch. iii., "The Reign of the Philosophers." Cf. also Hatch's *Hibbert Lectures*, Lects. II., IV., "Greek Education," "Greek and Christian Rhetoric."

fostered by the patronage of Hadrian and the Antonines, there now began what may be succinctly described as *the set literary defence* of Christianity. I do not concern myself here with the theology of the Apologists, which, in my view, has had scant enough justice done to it by Engelhardt, Harnack, and their followers,[1] but confine myself to what is implied in the very existence of such an Apology. It needs no elaborate proof to show that the character of the age, as I have just described it, powerfully affected the form of the Apology. It is conceded that Justin and the rest who represent this phase of Christian literature treat Christianity predominatingly as a "new philosophy"[2]—a fact which goes

[1] To this school the Apologists have lost the real meaning of Christianity, and reduced it to a *Moralismus*, or rational natural theology—a very unfair representation.

[2] Cf. *e.g.*, Justin, *Dialogue*, 8.

with the other, that most of these writers were philosophers or rhetoricians by training and profession. The literary and rhetorical stamp is, therefore, on all they write; the learning, the arts, the dialectic of the schools, the skill of the forensic pleader, are brought into play by them without stint or disguise. This is the side of the Apology commonly dwelt on, but there is another. The very appearance of such an Apology marks a great step in advance. It shows not only that the spirit of the age had affected Christianity, but also that Christianity had pushed its way into literary circles, and was attracting their attention. It makes clear that the Christians were beginning to have confidence in themselves, felt their growing power, were no longer content to be "a dumb folk, muttering in corners,"[1] as their enemies scornfully

[1] Min. Felix, 8, 31.

described them, but were emboldened to present their case in the open court of public opinion, and to challenge a verdict in their favour on the ground of its inherent reasonableness. There is a high tone in the writers of these Apologies which the reader cannot mistake. "They are always more or less conscious," as Baur says, "that they are the soul of the world, the substantial centre holding everything together, the pivot on which the world's history revolved, and those who alone have a future to look to. . . . When there are men," he adds, "who feel themselves in this way to be the soul of the world, the time is indisputably approaching when the reins of the government of the world will fall unasked into their hands."[2] The point of special interest to us in this connection is that, as I have already said, these writers— one and all—were men of liberal culture,

History of Church, II. pp. 129, 131 (E.T.).

of wide and varied learning, several of them philosophers by profession ; and they appear at a great variety of points scattered over the surface of the Church. Aristides, the author of the earliest complete Apology we possess—only the other year recovered— was a philosopher of Athens ; Athenagoras, in the reign of M. Aurelius, was also a philosopher of Athens ; from Athens, too, is said (though this is doubtful) to have come the oldest of all the Apologies— that of Quadratus. Justin Martyr passed through the Platonic and other schools of philosophy in his search for the truth, and after his conversion, continued to wear his philosopher's mantle, and to dispute in public places in Ephesus and Rome with any who would hear him. A man of learning like himself, though of widely different spirit, was his disciple Tatian — the author of the recently discovered *Diatessaron*.

Theophilus of Antioch, Melito of Sardis, Apolinarius of Hierapolis, were bishops, but men of culture and philosophic training, well acquainted with heathen systems. Minucius Felix, author of what Renan calls "the pearl of the apologetic literature of the reign of M. Aurelius,"[1] was a Roman advocate. Tertullian's learning, and legal and rhetorical gifts, I need not speak of. All this implies that Christianity had penetrated in no slight degree into the schools, and was exercising a powerful attraction on minds athirst for truth and certainty on the great questions of existence, as well as drawing into its service not a few of the gifted and earnest men of culture of the time.

With this rise of a literary Apology *for* Christianity must be connected a yet more significant phenomenon in the Pagan world —the rise of a formal literary *attack* on

[1] *Marc-Aurèle*, ch. xxii.

Christianity. It may be taken for granted that a religion must already have attracted considerable attention before the ablest literary men of the time sit down to write elaborate refutations of it. I remarked before that if M. Aurelius kept silence about the Christians it was not because he did not know enough regarding them. He was surrounded with people who knew them well. Fronto of Cirta, the celebrated rhetorician, one of his tutors, and an intimate correspondent and friend, wrote a bitter attack on the Christians, which Renan thinks is reproduced in the *Octavius* of Minucius Felix.[1] Diognetus, another of the tutors of Marcus, is probably the same to whom the beautiful *Epistle to Diognetus* is addressed. Herodes Atticus, yet another of his tutors, the wealthiest man and most famous orator of his time, had, as on the ground of a Cata-

[1] *Marc-Aurèle*, ch. xxii.

comb inscription we have seen reason to believe, a daughter who was a Christian. Rusticus, the prefect of Marcus, presided at the trial of Justin and his companions. The policy of silence was, besides, no longer observed. I have just mentioned Fronto's written attack. Lucian satirised the Christians in his witty *Peregrinus Proteus*, which is in truth an honourable tribute to their charity. Celsus wrote his *True Word* (λόγος ἀληθής) in refutation of their opinions.[1] It is this work of Celsus which, above all, shows how important a phenomenon Christianity was now felt to be, and how carefully the writings of the Christians were being studied by some of their opponents. Here is a man of undeniable acuteness, of wide reading, of

[1] Celsus' book has been largely reconstructed by Keim on the basis of the extracts and notices in Origen. There is a good sketch of it in Pressensé's *Martyrs and Apologists*, bk. iii.

EARLY PROGRESS OF CHRISTIANITY 193

philosophic culture, of exceptional literary ability, who of deliberate purpose sets himself down to assail, undermine, and overthrow Christianity by all the resources of knowledge, argument, and raillery, at his command. He sets about his work in no light spirit, but as one who feels that he must bend all his powers to attain his end. To fit himself for this task he makes a minute study of the Christian writings, keenly notes every assailable point, makes himself acquainted with the Christian beliefs, then, passing to the synagogue, gathers up all the slanders which Jewish malice could invent. It is fair to say that, like Pliny, he acquits the Christians of the grosser calumnies which were urged against them, but, short of this, he spares no pains to damage and discredit the sect. And we may be sure that in this desire to know something about the Christians and their literature Celsus did not stand alone. But even this clever opponent of Christianity cannot close his volume without giving us involuntarily a glimpse of the real situation. Having exhausted his artillery of argument and mockery, he betakes himself to something nearly approaching entreaty. "The conclusion of *The True Word*," says Dr. Bigg, " is creditable both to the sagacity and to the temper of its author. But when the persecutor thus found his weapons breaking in his grasp, and stooped to appeal to the generosity of his victim, it is evident that the battle was already lost."[1]

In yet another form, the same lesson of the powerful influence which Christianity was exercising on the thought and religion of the age is taught by those extraordinary and bewildering manifestations of religious phantasy which we ordinarily name Gnosti-

[1] *Platonists of Alex.*, p. 267. Cf. Uhlhorn's *Conflict of Christianity*, p. 279.

cism. Gnosticism is peculiarly the heresy of
the second century. We can best judge of
the scale of its influence, and the acuteness of
the crisis it evoked, by observing the extent
to which it bulks in the existing literature of
the period. The whole of Irenæus, a great
part of Tertullian, the whole of Hippolytus
nearly, and not a little of Clement of Alexandria, are devoted to its refutation. This
does not take account of lost treatises. But
we have only to consider the nature of this
singular appearance to see that it is one of
the most convincing testimonies we possess
to the power with which Christianity was
penetrating the innermost regions of thought
and speculation in the second century. This
is the side of the subject to which, as it seems
to me, justice has not always been done.
Harnack, *e.g.*, properly lays stress on Gnosticism as a phenomenon of the first importance
in the early Church. He hits off its charac-

teristic by describing it as an acute stage of that Hellenising of Christianity which afterwards was accomplished more gradually in the development of the Catholic dogma.[1] But, without discussing at present the justice of this view, it is surely obvious that if Gnosticism was on the one side an acute Hellenising—I should prefer to say Orientalising—of Christianity, it was not less on the other an acute Christianising of Hellenic and Oriental speculations. Gnosticism has this peculiarity, that it is the result of a blending of Christian ideas with the floating religious and theosophical speculations of the time, especially those derived from an Oriental, or a mixed Greek and Oriental, source. It was a product which did not spring up spontaneously in the minds of the mechanics and slaves and women and children, whom most, like Celsus, suppose to have formed the bulk of the Christian

[1] Cf. his *Hist. of Dogma*, I. p. 223 ff. (E.T.).

communities, but could only have taken its rise in minds of a more cultured and speculative cast. This, indeed, was its claim—to be a religion of "Gnosis," or knowledge, for the more highly trained or *élite*. It could only exist at all, therefore, as the result of a Christian ferment which had entered these speculative circles, and was there powerfully at work. Baur rightly appreciates the situation when he says:—"Gnosticism gives the clearest proof that Christianity had now come to be one of the most important factors in the history of the time, and it shows especially what a mighty power of attraction the new Christian principles possessed for the highest intellectual life then to be found either in the Pagan or in the Jewish world."[1] Above all, these systems are a striking witness to the impression produced on the heathen mind by the great Christian idea

[1] *Hist. of Church*, II. p. 1 (E.T.).

of Redemption. "When the Gnostic systems," says Neander, "describe the movement which was produced in the kingdom of the Demiurge by the appearance of Christ as the manifestation of a new and mighty principle which had entered the precincts of this lower world, they give us to understand how powerful was the impression which the contemplation of the life of Christ, and of His influence on humanity, had left on the minds of the founders of these systems, making all earlier institutions seem to them as nothing in comparison with Christianity."[1] We must beware, therefore, of underestimating either the extent or the intensity of this great intellectual ferment set up by the gospel in the heart of heathenism. The Gnostic sects multiplied with extraordinary rapidity, and the influence exercised by their most renowned teachers, as Basilides

[1] *Hist. of Church,* II. p. 8 (Bohn).

EARLY PROGRESS OF CHRISTIANITY 199

and Valentinus, was exceptionally great. The Church of the Marcionites—only, however, partially Gnostic—long maintained its ground as an independent ecclesiastical organisation.[1]

From the phenomena just considered in the sphere of the Church, we turn now to survey briefly certain scarcely less striking facts which meet us on the 'ground of Paganism. It is well understood that the second century was an age of ethical and religious revival; but it is not always realised how powerful this current of revival was, and how remarkable were some of the forms which it assumed. I have said that this age of the Antonines was an age of lecturing, preaching, teaching, and declaiming, beyond all precedent. From the time of Vespasian the Empire had been provided with a hierarchy of rhetoricans and grammarians, whose business

[1] Cf. *Dict. of Christ. Biog.*, III. p. 819.

it was to instruct the people in all liberal arts; and society was overrun with professional talkers, debaters, moralists, ready to supply oratory on any subject to whoever cared to pay for it. There was little in this sophistic declamation to make the world wiser and better; yet it is undeniable that towards the end of the first, and during the course of the second century, a certain glow of moral enthusiasm began to spread itself through the Empire, accompanied by a manifest revival of religious faith and earnestness.[1] In some of its representatives this fervour rose almost to a kind of Apostolic zeal. "It is too often forgotten," says Renan, "that the second century had a veritable Pagan preaching similar to that of Christianity, and in many respects in accord with the latter."[2]

[1] On this religious revival in the second century, see Friedländer, *Sittengeschichte*, III. pp. 430-33; Bigg's *Christian Platonists of Alex.*, pp. 23 ff.

[2] *Marc-Aurèle*, chap. iii. p. 45. Cf. Lightfoot, *Ignatius*, p. 449.

An early type of this species of "itinerant homilists," as Merivale names them, "who began from the Flavian period to go about proclaiming moral truths, collecting groups of hearers, and sowing the seeds of spiritual wisdom and knowledge on every soil that could receive it,"[1] was Apollonius of Tyana, to whose gifts of teaching was added the repute of miraculous powers.[2] Other and loftier types of this Pagan ministry are the celebrated Dion Chrysostom,[3] in the reigns of Nerva and Trajan, and Maximus of Tyre

[1] *Romans under the Empire*, chap. lxvi.

[2] His life, with romantic embellishments, was written by Philostratus at the request of the Empress Julia Domna, A.D. 217. See Newman's sketch of it in his *Life of Apollonius Tyanæus*, and Bigg's *Christian Platonists*, pp. 243-247.

[3] On *Dion*, eighty of whose orations remain to us, see the interesting sketch in Merivale, *Romans under the Empire*, chap. lxvi. "The name of Chrysostom," he says, "may have already reminded us of the most illustrious of the ancient Christian orators, and his speeches, of which large numbers are preserved,

under the Antonines.[1] Epictetus, the greatest name in the history of Stoicism after Seneca, is the noblest representative of the movement on its earnest philosophic side. With all this went on, as the accompaniment and counterpart of these better features, a vast development of superstition, an inrush of Oriental cults, a craving for theurgy and mysteries, a general susceptibility to dupery, giving rise to such characters as Alexander of Abonotichus, the most stupendous example, perhaps, of successful charlatanry in history.[2]

---

may be compared, with little disadvantage, with the sermons of the Bishop of Constantinople, for their warm appeals both to the heart and the conscience of their hearers."

[1] Forty-one orations of Maximus are preserved. On him and the others see Hatch, *Hibbert Lectures*, pp. 6–242, &c. The sketch of Ælius in Friedländer, III. p. 440, may also be consulted.

[2] Cf. Froude's "A Cagliostro of the Second Century" in *Short Studies*, vol. iv. In this and other sketches in vols. iii. and iv., Froude gives admirable characterisations of the period.

What, now, are we to say of this remarkable revival movement in second century heathenism, and, in particular, can it be affirmed that Christianity had anything to do with it? The majority of writers would probably answer—No. I cannot, however, share this view. It seems to me *primâ facie* unreasonable that, in summing up the forces which helped to give the age its character, we should take account of every stray influence from East to West—of Epicureanism, of Stoicism, of Pythagoreanism, of Isis- and Mithras-worship, of an Apollonius of Tyana, of a Dion Chrysostom, of charlatans even like Alexander of Abonotichus; but that no influence whatever should be attributed, or allowed, to this constantly present and intensely active force of the Christian religion. It is true that Christianity was persecuted, was regarded with contempt and scorn, but we must not be deceived by this into supposing that its influence was not telling silently and secretly on multitudes in the Empire, and that it was not affecting Paganism in many indirect ways, even where the obligation to it was not openly acknowledged. We saw before that Epictetus alludes to it but once, and with contempt, but there is good reason for believing that he was not unacquainted with its Scriptures or uninfluenced by its teaching.

I believe that we profoundly err in assuming that the borrowing of ideas and moulding of institutions in this age was all on the part of the Christian Church, and that a very considerable influence was not going out also from the Christian Church on the religion and life of Paganism. Dr. Hatch, for instance, would see in the lecturing and declaiming of this rhetorical age the origin of the Christian sermon.[1] But might we not, with

[1] *Hibbert Lectures*, p. 113.

equal reason, reverse the supposition? Is it not, at least, as likely that the example of the Christian Church, its unceasing and intensely zealous propaganda, extending now over more than a century, and presenting so splendid an example of success, had something to do with kindling the enthusiasm and quickening the Apostolic zeal of such itinerant preachers as Dion and Maximus? Take the picture of that Christian propaganda as furnished by so sober a pen as Friedländer's. "The example of the first Apostles," he says, " unceasingly stirred up imitators in constantly increasing number, who, according to the doctrine of the gospel, shared their possessions with the poor, and grasped the travelling-staff in order to carry the Word of God from people to people, and whose zeal neither wearied nor grew cold under the greatest difficulties and dangers. The Christians were zealous (says

Origen) to sow the seed of the Word in the whole world. The messengers of the new doctrine visited not only cities, but also villages and farms; nay, did not shun to force themselves into the interior of families, and to place themselves between those related by blood."[1] The success which attended this zealous gospel preaching in Rome, in Bithynia, in Carthage, in Antioch, everywhere, we have already seen, and it was a constant object-lesson to the Pagans, who felt their own faith crumbling, and were looking round for means with which to combat the victorious progress of the new religion which emptied their temples, and made even the purchase of sacrifices to cease. Can we believe, then, that it had nothing to do with awakening their emulation, and inciting them to a similar propa-

[1] *Sittengeschichte,* III. p. 517.

gandism?[1] Their silence and contempt go for nothing. When Maximin[2] and Julian conceived the idea of re-modelling the Pagan priesthood as a set-off to the Christian hierarchy, they did not proclaim in so many words that it was this hated sect they were imitating, any more than the Anglican Church, when the Evangelical Revival was pouring new life into its veins, made public acknowledgment of its indebtedness to Wesley and Whitefield. In a similar way, it is no disproof of the manifold influences with which Christianity was bathing the Paganism of the second century, that the recipients of the benefit do not acknowledge

[1] Merivale points out that Dion Chrysostom had probably a connection with Flavius Clemens, the consul, who suffered for his faith under Domitian.

[2] Cf. Euseb. ix. 4. "Maximin perceived the power that existed in the Catholic Church with its wonderful organisation, and conceived the stupendous idea of rejuvenating Paganism by creating a Pagan Catholic Church" (McGiffert's note).

the source from which it comes. We see the change that is in process; we mark the new spirit and the energetic propaganda; we know that this has come into existence with the example of the Christian Church before it, and the influences of the Christian faith permeating every pore of the old system; and we think it not unreasonable to suppose that there is a connection between the facts.

This influence of Christianity which we indicate is probable in itself, and the presumption in its favour is strengthened when we consider certain other features in the religious condition of the age, which it is difficult to avoid tracing in some measure to Christian influence. It has been hinted above that the second century was an age not only of ethical, but of religious revival. It was an age characterised by a new sense of sin and weakness, by a longing for redemption from these evils, by a yearning for immediate communion with the Deity, by the craving for the assurance of a blessed life hereafter. Outwardly, it was marked by a great influx of foreign cults, and specially by the introduction of new forms of heathen mysteries, and the extraordinary development and rapid spread of the latter. The chief were those of the Phrygian Cybele, of the Egyptian Isis and Osiris, and of the Persian Mithras—the types which promised most satisfaction to the cravings referred to.[1] The effects of these mysteries on the ideas and usages of the Christian Church have been traced by Dr. Hatch and others, not without some exaggeration,[2] but

[1] Cf. on this subject of the mysteries, Boissier's *La Religion Romaine*, bk. ii., chap. ii. ; Anrich's *Die Antike Mysterienwesen*; Hatch's *Hibbert Lectures*, x. ; Cheetham's *Mysteries : Pagan and Christian* ; Bigg's *Christian Platonists*. The older and newer literature may be seen in Cheetham.

[2] Cheetham's book deals with some instances of this.

the counter-question of a possible influence of Christianity on the mysteries has received but scant attention. Yet I believe there is an important field to be worked here also. The mysteries, especially those which sprang up in the time of the Empire, deserve the closest study we can give them. They represent, as Renan has said, the most serious phase of Pagan religion—are, in a sense, the underground Church of Heathenism. But it is necessary also to study them with discrimination, and to distinguish carefully times and seasons, and the successive stages of development. When we do this, we discover that the special period of growth of these new cults is from the second century onwards[1]; that there are

[1] "This new development of the mysteries," says Anrich, "is conditioned by the re-awakening of the religious life which exhibits its slight beginnings in the first century, in order from that steadily to increase, till in the third century this new type of

certain ground-features in which they all agree; but that their distinctive forms, rites, and terminology are often a later formation, and are strongly affected by the conditions of the age. Among these conditions we do not think it unreasonable that the Christian Church—the most formidable rival of the mysteries in the Empire—should be included. It is certain that the Fathers of the Church held the mysteries in abhorrence, and that whatever borrowing took place from these on the Christian side was unconscious, and in a sense involuntary.[1]

religious tendency, essentially different from the piety of earlier times, has become the all-controlling power of the age " (p. 35). He observes how the Isis-cult had a rapid development after the middle of the second century, and in the third century "was perhaps most widely spread, and at all events the most important religion of the Roman Empire," and how the Mithras-cult, which begins to spread in the first century "reached, however, first in the age of Diocletian and Constantine its highest bloom" (pp. 43-45).

[1] Anrich, p. 235 ; Cheetham, p. 78.

But it is not so unlikely that the patrons of the mysteries should adopt terms and features from the language and worship of the Christian Church. And that they actually did so seems the simplest explanation of various striking facts. I may refer to the prominence given in the later mysteries to the idea of the σωτήρ, and the description of the promised blessing as σωτηρία [1]—for though these terms are not new in Paganism, they are brought into new connections, and acquire a deeper significance in the age we are speaking of. So again, we have the use of such terms as *renatus*, or *renatus in eternum*,[2] to designate the initiated person; we have new expiatory rites, culminating in the hideous Taurobolium [3]; we

[1] Cf. Anrich, pp. 47, 49. Mithras came to be called σωτήρ. On the older usage, see Cheetham, p. 15.

[2] See passages in Anrich, pp. 47, 53, &c.

[3] Ibid. pp. 51–2 ; cf. Bigg, pp. 238.

have curious resemblances to the Christian Sacraments,[1] which the early Christian writers could only explain by supposing that the demons had invented a caricature of Christian ordinances with the view of throwing discredit on the latter[2]; we have the further developments of the initiation of very young children—a sort of infant baptism[3]—and, in general, the growth of something like a Church idea in these secret celebrations.[4] When we remember the hold taken on Gnostic minds by the ideas of the σωτήρ and of redemption, and reflect on the half-pagan character and wide diffusion of many of the Gnostic sects, we may

[1] Cf. Harnack, as below. These resemblances were chiefly in the Mithras-cult.

[2] Cf. Justin, *Apol.* i. 66 ; Tert. *De Præs. Hær.*, 40; and see Harnack, *Hist. of Dogma*, I. p. 118 (E.T.).

[3] Anrich, p. 55.

[4] Ibid., p. 56. "The worship of Mithras in the third century," says Dr. Harnack, "became the most powerful rival of Christianity" (I. p. 118, E.T.).

perhaps—even apart from the direct influence of the Church—see a channel through which the ideas of Christianity might filter into purely Pagan circles. Dr. Bigg, in his lectures on *The Christian Platonists of Alexandria* has some suggestive remarks on this point, which are, I think, in the main correct. " The disciples of Mithra," he says, " formed an organised hierarchy. They possessed the ideas of mediation, atonement, and a Saviour, who is human and yet divine, and not only the idea, but a doctrine of the future life. They had a Eucharist and a baptism, and other curious analogies might be pointed out between their system and the Church of Christ. Most of these conceptions, no doubt, are integral parts of a religion much older than Christianity [some of them on the other hand do not seem to go beyond the second or third century]. But when we consider how strange they are to the older polytheism of Greece and Rome, and when we observe further that Mithraism did not come into vogue till the time of Hadrian, that is to say, till the age of Gnosticism, we shall hardly be wrong in judging that resemblances were pushed forward, exaggerated, modified with a special view to the necessities of the conflict with the new faith, and that differences, such as the barbarous superstitions of the Avesta, were kept sedulously in the background with the same object. Paganism was copying Christianity, and by that very act was lowering her arms."[1]

Fully to estimate the force of these considerations, it is necessary to bear in mind the evidence which has already been adduced as to the extent to which Christianity had penetrated literary circles, and had become known to learned opponents, who employed

[1] P. 240; cf. Cheetham, pp. 77, 146.

their best abilities to discredit and destroy it
—in vain.

Much might be said of the writings of the old Catholic Fathers, and especially of the famed Alexandrian school, in illustration of the subject we are considering. For how clear is the evidence in the writings of these Fathers of the hold that Christianity had taken of men of the most powerful intelligence and widest learning; how plain the indications that it had become a subject of the profoundest theological reflection; how complete its victory over the brilliant *Aufklärung* of Gnosticism; how evident the alliance which had been effected between it and the best elements of the Greek wisdom— that revelation in reason which the Alexandrian Fathers, with Justin, traced to the illumination of the pre-incarnate Logos! If the school of Harnack sees in the theologica movement of this period an amalgamation of

Greek intellectualism with Christianity, it must in consistency recognise that the prevailing Greek spirit had been seized and was being led captive by the new faith. And that of itself speaks to a mighty internal force of assimilation. Without, however, dwelling on this, I hasten to speak of what is, after all, perhaps the most striking proof of the influence of these Fathers of the Early Church on contemporary religious thought—I mean the rise of Neo-Platonism in the third century. In this century, as we previously saw, the river whose course we have been tracing flows no longer underground, but comes to the light of open day. The fact of a Christian influence on the intellectual currents of the age is all too patent to be further denied. I referred in the previous lecture to the eclectic temper of this age, and to its characteristic embodiments in Julia Domna, the talented wife of the Emperor Septimus Severus, and in Alexander Severus, a succeeding emperor. Julia Domna gathered round her at her court a brilliant literary circle. It was at her command that Philostratus wrote the "Life of Apollonius"[1]—partly, there is reason to believe, as a parallel to the representation of the life of Jesus in the Gospels. Alexander Severus went further, and, as formerly narrated, placed the statue of Christ along with those of Abraham, Pythagoras, and others in his lararium, besides inscribing the Golden Rule on his walls and monuments. "Men sought," says Dr. Bigg, "to distil an elixir from all religions, from all, that is, except Christianity, which they never name"—a statement which needs to be slightly qualified. "Yet," he goes on, "the church from which they avert their eyes as from the angel

[1] Cf. *Classical Dictionary*, Art. "Philostratus"; Newman's *Apollonius Tyanæus*; Bigg's *Christian Platonists*, p. 246.

of doom, is really the prompter and guide of all their efforts."[1] Under these intellectual and spiritual conditions, arose the new form of opposition to Christianity which we denominate Neo-Platonism. The founder of this school, Ammonius Saccas—whose lectures Origen for a time attended at Alexandria—was born of Christian parents, and, indeed, for a time himself professed Christianity.[2] Here is proof, if such were needed, of a strain of Christian influence entering into Neo-Platonism at the commencement. Ammonius, it should be remarked, had an important precursor in the second century, Numenius, who likewise was moulded by Jewish and Christian influences.[3] The ideas of the founder were developed by his more

[1] *Christian Platonists*, p. 242.
[2] Eusebius, *Ecc. Hist.* vi. 19. Eusebius will not admit that he ever apostatised, but this is evidently a mistake.
[3] Cf. Bigg, pp. 251-3.

famous pupil Plotinus, and carried still further by the third great teacher Porphyry. The Neo-Platonic system thus developed, while bitterly hostile to Christianity, is really the strongest testimony to its power. It not only shows upon itself the distinct mark of Christian ideas—*e.g.* in its doctrine of the Trinity, respecting which Bigg truly remarks —" It may be confidently affirmed that no Trinity is to be found in any Pagan philosopher who was not well acquainted with Christianity "[1]; it was not only, as Schaff has observed, " a direct attempt of the more intelligent and earnest heathenism to rally all its nobler energies, especially the forces of Hellenic and Oriental Mysticism, and to found a universal religion, a Pagan counterpart to the Christian "[2]; but it testifies to the changed attitude towards Christianity in the

[1] Cf. Bigg, p. 250.
[2] *Church Hist.* (Ante-Nic.), p. 99.

fact that it no longer poured unqualified ridicule on the new religion as Celsus had done, but dealt with it rather in the philosophical eclectic spirit characteristic of the time, condemning only its exclusive claims. It reckoned Christ among the sages; professed respect for His personal teaching, as contrasted with the corrupted doctrines of His Apostles, and sought to appropriate its spiritual elements to itself. "The Neo-Platonists," says Augustine, "praised Christ, while they disparaged Christianity." "We must not," said Porphyry himself, "calumniate Christ, but only those who worship Him as God."[1] But the battle was a hopeless one. "Under the banner of Neo-Platonism," says Dr. Lightfoot, "and with weapons forged in the armoury of Christianity itself, the contest is renewed. But the day of heathenism is past. This new

[1] Augustine, *City of God*, xix. 23.

champion retires from the field of conflict in confusion, and the gospel remains in possession of the field."[1]

Here I must close. Other parts of the field I am compelled to leave well-nigh untouched, especially that relating to the influence of Christianity on social life and legislation. This, at the same time, is the part of the subject which has been least neglected. It has often been shown with abundance of illustration how revolutionary were the ideas and principles of the holy and spiritual religion which had its birth in Judæa when introduced into the unspeakably corrupt society of the Græco-Roman Empire.[2] To the profligacy of that effete heathen world, Christianity opposed its own fresh, young life, and glowing spiritual ideals; to its pride,

[1] *Philippians*, p. 319.
[2] Cf. the works of Troplong, Schmidt, Uhlhorn, Lecky, Loring Brace, with the histories of Milman, Pressensé, Schaff, &c.

EARLY PROGRESS OF CHRISTIANITY 223

the proclamation of a common fall and a common salvation ; to its selfish egoism, the demand for a universal charity ; to its denial of the rights of humanity, the doctrine of the love of God, and of the spiritual dignity of man as made in the image of God ; to its degradation of woman, the assertion that in Christ Jesus there is neither Jew nor Greek, male nor female, bond nor free[1] ; to its contempt for labour, the recollection of the Carpenter, and the injunction " Take thought for things honourable in the sight of all men."[2] Opposed at nearly every point to the existing Pagan order, it yet gave to the world of that time exactly what it needed, implanted within it the seeds of emancipation and renewal. If it could not save the old Roman Empire, it at least laid within it the foundations on which the rearing of a new order could proceed—

Gal. iii. 28.   [2] Rom. xii. 17.

rendered possible the rise of a rejuvenated and progressive Europe. The pure morals and blameless, self-denying lives of the Christians, were the strongest points the Apologists for the new religion could urge in its favour. Thus Tertullian powerfully contrasts the private virtues and public morality of his fellow-believers with the foul conduct of the Pagans, and challenges his opponents to produce instances of Christians in the long list of those committed to prison for their crimes.[1] If there were exceptions, it was only as it must happen to the healthiest and purest body, that a mole should grow, or a wart arise on it, or freckles disfigure it.[2] The heathen themselves bore involuntary testimony to the superior excellence of the Christian character by appealing to it in rebuke of the lack of virtue in one another.[3]

[1] *Apol.*, 42–46 ; *Ad Nat.* i. 4.   [2] *Ad Nat.* i. 5.
[3] " You are accustomed in conversation yourselves

EARLY PROGRESS OF CHRISTIANITY 225

As respects legislation, naturally little could be done till the Empire had become publicly Christian, but with Constantine we have already numerous enactments which show the new spirit that had entered society,[1] and under the succeeding emperors these evidences of Christian influence are multiplied.[2] The Theodosian code is little more than a compilation of the decisions of the Christian emperors. Even in the earlier period, it is not wholly unreasonable to see in the gradual ameliorations introduced into many of the laws under the influence of the newer Stoicism an indirect result, at least in part,

to say, why is so-and-so so deceitful, when the Christians are so self-denying? why merciless, when they are so merciful?" &c.—*Ad Nat.* i. 5.

[1] Julian termed Constantine, "Novator turbatorque priscarum legum et moris antiquitus recepti" (Amm. Marc. xxi. 10). See a sketch of his reforms in the laws relating to women, children, slaves, &c., in *Dict. of Christ. Biog.* I. pp. 636–7.

[2] See Loring Brace's *Gesta Christi*, passim.

of that atmosphere of mercy with which the Christian Church was already bathing Paganism.[1]

In leaving the subject, I can only express the hope that these lectures, however imperfect, may have done something to intensify our sense of the mighty power which, as the Divine Leaven introduced into humanity, Christianity from its first entrance into the world exercised on everything it touched, and to guard against the tendency, still too prevalent, unduly to minimise its influence.

[1] Cf. Troplong, *L'Influence du Christ.*, p. 83, &c.

APPENDIX

NOTE ON THE INSCRIPTIONS OF THE ACILII

(*in Frontispiece*).

FOR the drawings of these inscriptions, I am indebted to the Rev. Archibald Paterson, B.D., Rosslyn, who from his first-hand researches kindly furnished me with information regarding them. They should, he thinks, probably be restored and identified as follows:—

1.

ACILIO GLABRIONI		ACILIO GLABRIONI
FILIO	*or*	FILIO
M' ACILII GLABRIONIS		M' ACILIUS GLABRIO
COS.		PATER.

Deceased may have been the son of Manius Acilius Glabrio, consul in A.D. 124, the latter probably being the son of the consul of A.D. 91, who suffered under Domitian, in A.D. 95.

2.

MANIUS ACILIUS VERUS
CLARISSIMUS VIR,

ET (?) PRISCILLA CLARISSIMA $\begin{cases} \text{PUELLA (?)} \\ \text{FEMINA (?)} \end{cases}$

May be the children of Manius Acilius Glabrio, consul in A.D. 152 [son of the consul of A.D. 124], and Vera Priscilla, who is known from an inscription to have been the wife of a Manius Acilius Glabrio. The Manius Acilius Glabrio who was her husband may, however, have been the consul of this name in A.D. 186 [son of the consul of A.D. 152]. In this case the children will be *their* offspring.

3.

A fragment probably of—

ACILIA
M[ARCI] ACILII,

belonging to the family of Marcus Acilius Vibius

APPENDIX 229

Faustinus, who was one of the Salii before A.D. 170; or to the family of Marcus Acilius Priscus Egrilius Plarianus, who lived at the same time.

4.

Κλανδιον Ακειλιον Ουαλεριον [λαμπροτατον] νεανισκον.

It is known that Claudius Acilius Cleoboles (grandson of the consul of A.D. 186) derived his name Claudius from adoption by Tiberius Claudius Cleoboles, consul suffectus (year uncertain). The name Valerius is from the mother's side. The inscription cannot be earlier than the third century.

INDEX

ABERCIUS, of Hieropolis, 54
Acilius Glabrio, consul, 125 ff. ; inscriptions of Acilii, frontispiece, and appendix, 227
Ælius Aristides, 167, 202
Alexandria, Church of, 31, 60 ; mixed state of, 66–7 ; school in, 68, 216 ; wealth of, 140 ff.
Alexander Severus, emperor, 147, 218
Alexander of Abonotichus, 51, 202–3
Ambrose, of Milan, 158
Ammonius Saccas, 219
Anrich, on Mysteries, 209–13, *passim*
Antioch, Church of, its numbers, 73–83
Apollonius, senator, 137, 146
Apology, of 2nd century, 34, 58 ; its significance, 185–90 ; 224
Aristides, apology of, 45
Armenia, conversion of, 88

BAUR, 15 ; on apologists, 188 ; on Gnosticism, 197
Bigg, C., 146, 194–5, 209–20, *passim*
Bithynia - Pontus, Pliny's testimony, 48 ff. ; 129, 206
Blandina, martyr, 137
Boissier, G., on spread of Christianity, 27ff.; ignoring of Christianity by pagans, 168, 170 ; influence of Christianity, 175, 183
Brace, Loring, on influence of Christianity, 19, 225

CÆCILIA, St., *see* Catacombs.
Catacombs, character and

INDEX

extent of, 35 ff. ; testimony to numbers of Christians, 33–5, 39–41 ; inscriptions, 98 ; testimony to wealth of Christians, 113 ff., 132 ff. ; cemeteries of Lucina, 118; of Domitilla, 123 ; of the Acilii, 126 (with frontispiece and appendix) ; of Prætextatus, 132 ; of Cæcilia, 134 ff.

Cappadocia, Church in, 56

Caracalla, emperor, 146

Carthage, Church of, 30 ; numbers, 61 ff. ; rank and wealth, 139–43 ; martyrdom of Perpetua, 143–4 ; 206

Celsus, his *True Word*, 59, 71, 99, 167, 192–4 ; 196, 221

Chastel, on nos. of Christians, 24

Cheetham, on Mysteries, 209–12

Christianity, influence of paganism on, 18, 163, 204, 209 ; effects of Christianity on paganism, 20 ff. ; on pagan preaching, 204 ff. ; on Mysteries, 210 ff. ; on morals and legislation, 222 ff.

Chrysostom, on Church of Antioch, 75 ff.; 158

Churches in Rome, Corinth, Ephesus, Galatia, Antioch, Bithynia, Pontus, Cyrene, Alexandria, Carthage, Gaul, Spain, &c.— *See* under these heads.

Claudius, emperor, his edict, 42

Clement, of Rome, 43

Clement, of Alexandria, on luxury of Christians, 141–2 ; Gnosticism, 195 ; 216

Commodus, emperor, 145

Corinth, Church of, 32, 107, 108–9, 130, 171–2

Cyprian, of Carthage, 86, 151, 158

Cyrene, Church in, 31

DECIAN PERSECUTION, 86, 149 ff.

De Rossi, G. B., on Catacombs, 34, 117, 123, 135, 175, 179, 183

De Rossi, Michele, measurements of, 37 ff.

Diocletian, emperor, persecution of, 87 ff. ; 152 ff.

Dion Chrysostom, 201, 205

Dionysius, of Alexandria, 148, 150, 158

Domitilla, Flavia, 122 ff.; cemetery of, 123

Domitian, emperor, persecution of, 121 ff.

INDEX

ELAGABULUS, emperor, 147
Elvira, Council of, 86, 157
Emperors, *see* under names.
Ephesus, Church of, 44, 108, 171-2
Epictetus, 183, 204
Eusebius, references to, 48, 51, 54, 56, 59, 73-4, 78, 82, 87-90, 123, 130, 137, 145-6, 148, 152-3, 154-6, 207

FARRAR, F. W., 141, 177
Flavius Clemens, consul, his martyrdom, 122 ff.
Friedlander, on numbers of Christians, 24, 116 ; on obscurity of Church, 165-6 ; 177, 179, 183, 200, 202 ; on the Christian propaganda, 205
Froude, J. A. 202

GALATIA, Church in, 55, 57, 171
Gaul, Christianity in, 30, 81 ff.
Gibbon, on numbers of Christians, 24, 39, 68, 78 ff. ; 47, 51, 122
Gnosticism, 58, 184, 194 ff., 213, 215-16
Greek Spirit and Christianity, 17, 164, 187, 196
Gregory Thaumaturgus, 52, 158

HADRIAN, emperor, 66-8
Harnack, quoted, 116, 124, 133, 163, 213 ; referred to, 118, 123, 128, 164, 195, 216
Hasenclever, on rank of Christians, 64, 118 ; 177
Hatch, E., 16, 185, 202, 204, 209
Hefele, on Councils, 84, 86
Hermas, on Roman Church, 130
Herod Atticus, 133, 191-2

IGNATIUS, 59, 73, 129
Imperial Court, Christianity in the, 116, 124, 145 ff.
Irenæus, of Lyons, 59, 64, 82, 146, 195

JULIA DOMNA, her influence, 146, 217
Julian, emperor, 74, 77, 207, 225
Justin Martyr, on spread of Christianity, 47 ; on wealth of Church, 132 ; as apologist, 186-9 ; 192, 213, 216

KEIM, on progress of Christianity, 27

LANCIANI, on Catacombs, 36 ff., 115, 123, 133, 134, 152 ; on Hadrian, 68
Lightfoot, Bishop, referred to or quoted, 16, 43, 45,

48, 50, 54, 55, 58, 67, 116, 118, 121–3, 126–7, 129, 130, 134–5, 173, 177–80, 182, 221
Lucian, of Antioch, martyr, on diffusion of Christianity, 90
Lucian, on Pontus, 51; his *Peregrinus Proteus*, 192
Lyons, its importance, 82–3; martyrdoms, 82, 136

MARCUS AURELIUS, emperor, 133, 189; relations to Christianity, 166, 171, 191
Martyrdoms, of Ignatius, Polycarp, Justin, at Vienne and Lyons, Perpetua, &c., *see* under names.
Maximin, emperor, his persecution and letter, 89, 207
Maximus, of Tyre, 201–2, 205
Merivale, referred to or quoted, 32, 112–13, 133, 169, 185, 201
Milman, 82, 90, 142
Mithras-cult, 209, 211–13, 215
Mommsen, 50, 55, 85, 116
Mosheim, 47
Mysteries, in Roman Empire, 209; possible influence of Christianity on, 210 ff.

NEANDER, 155, 198
Neo-Platonism, 149, 217 ff.
Nero, emperor, persecution of, 43; his palace, 116, 175
Neumann, 17, 42, 64, 138
Northcote and Brownlow, on Catacombs, 36 ff., 114 ff., 132 ff.

ORIGEN, on numbers of Christians, 68 ff.; intelligence of, 98–9, 144; relations with Court, 145–9, 158, 219

PAGANISM, ethical revival in, 199 ff.; pagan preaching, 200–2; religious revival, 208 ff.
Pamphilus, of Cæsarea, 158
Paul and Thecla, Acts of, 128
Perpetua and her companions, 143 ff.
Persecutions under Nero, Domitian, Trajan, Marcus Aurelius, Severus, Decius, Valerian, Diocletian, Maximin, *see* these names.
Phrygia, Christianity in, 53, 88
Pliny, correspondence with Trajan, 28, 48 ff., 129, 167–8, 193
Pomponia Græcina, 117, 136, 179

INDEX

Pontus, 51
Porphyry, 220-1
Pudens and Claudia, 119-21

RAMSAY, W. M., referred to or quoted, 17, 31, 42, 48, 53-5, 96, 105, 116, 128, 167-8, 182

Renan, 53, 83, 191, 200, 210
Ritschl, 16
Robertson, Canon, 27
Roman Empire, population of, 24-5, 29
Rome, Church of, 41-44, 78-9, 129-36, 137, 139, 206. *See* Catacombs.

SCHAFF, PHILIP, 34, 38, 220
Schultze, Vict., 31, 32 ; on numbers of Christians, 24-5, 43, 51, 56-7, 65, 75, 83-6 ; on rank of Christians, 99, 112
Seneca, relation to Christianity, 175 ff. ; Epistle to Lucilius, 180
Septimus Severus, emperor, persecution of, 138 ff. ; 146

Silence of Pagan writers on Christianity : how accounted for, 166 ff.
Social rank of Christ's personal disciples, 100 ff. ; of early converts, 104 ff.
Spain, Church in, 85 ff., 157

TACITUS, 28, 43, 117
Tertullian, on numbers of Christians, 28, 61 ff.; rank of, 139, 141-2 ; on Gnosticism, 195 ; the Mysteries, 213, 31, 48, 84, 86, 147, 224
Trajan, emperor, persecution under, 48, 129
Tryphæna, Queen, 128

UHLHORN, 26, 59, 146, 194
Urania, daughter of Herod Atticus, 133, 192

VALERIAN, emperor, persecution of, 148, 151
Vienne and Lyons, martyrdoms, 82, 136

WITHROW, 38, 116

www.ingramcontent.com/pod-product-compliance
Lightning Source LLC
Chambersburg PA
CBHW070312230426
43663CB00011B/2091